Guide to the

ANSI/NISO/LBI Library Binding Standard

ANSI/NISO/LBI Z39.78-2000

Jan Merrill-Oldham and Paul Parisi

Illustrations by Gary Frost

Preservation and Reformatting Section

Association for Library Collections & Technical Services

a division of the

American Library Association

Chicago 2008

Association for Library Collections & Technical Services, ALCTS, a division of the American Library Association, 50 E. Huron St., Chicago, IL 60611
www.ala.org/alcts

Printed in the United States of America.

11 10 09 -08- 4 3 2 1

ISBN: 978-0-8389-8484-0

Library of Congress Cataloging-in-Publication Data

Merrill-Oldham, Jan, 1947-
Guide to the ANSI/NISO/LBI library binding standard / Jan Merrill-Oldham and Paul ParisI ; illustrations by Gary Frost.
p. cm.
Updates the Guide to the Library Binding Institute standard for library binding. Chicago : American Library Association, 1990.
ISBN 978-0-8389-8484-0
1. Bookbinding--Standards--United States. 2. Library materials--Conservation and restoration--Standards--United States. 3. Books--Conservation and restoration--Standards--United States. I. Parisi, Paul A. II. Merrill-Oldham, Jan, 1947- Guide to the Library Binding Institute standard for library binding. III. Library Binding Institute. IV. National Information Standards Organization (U.S.) V. American National Standards Institute. VI. Association for Library Collections & Technical Services. Preservation and Reformatting Section VII. Title.
Z700.M48 2006
025.7--dc22

2008030044

www.ala.org/alcts

Contents

NOTE

This *Guide to the ANSI/NISO/LBI Library Binding Standard* supersedes the 1990 publication, *Guide to the Library Binding Institute Standard for Library Binding.*

Illustrations

Preface

Sixteen years have passed since the *Guide to the Library Binding Institute Standard for Library Binding* (the *Guide*) was published as a companion to the eighth edition of the *Library Binding Institute Standard for Library Binding* (*LBI Standard*).[1] An outgrowth of the interests of preservationists in the American Library Association (ALA), the *Guide* explained and illustrated the *LBI Standard* and pointed out areas where uncertainty or disagreement existed within the industry. Compromise, rather than consensus characterized some parts of the document.

We returned to the *Guide* in 2006 with the intention of bringing its numbering scheme into harmony with the current version of the *ANSI/NISO/LBI Z39.78-2000, Library Binding Standard.*[2] Our plan was to alter a few sentences here and there to reflect the developments in manufacturing that have occurred since the *Guide* was first issued. As we reviewed the text, however, we made a surprising discovery. Although we were well aware of each change that had taken place in the industry in recent years, it became evident to us that nearly all of the concerns raised by librarians and binders throughout the 1970s and '80s had been addressed comprehensively by the industry.

Consider the library binding landscape in 1986. Oversewing was the cornerstone of the business and had been for more than fifty years. Double-fan adhesive binding was robust enough to merit its inclusion in the 1986 edition of the *LBI Standard* as a mainstream option, but the process had not been tested and there were no commercially manufactured, double-fan adhesive binding machines available for purchase. Spine notching was allowed, but the technique had not been tested and its adoption was not widespread. Group F buckram, the covering material used for nearly all library bindings, was often criticized for being too thick, stiff, and shiny. Questions about trimming text blocks, using the proper adhesive for the proper purpose, treating the spines of text blocks or the corners of covers, reinforcing endcaps, and manufacturing cover board had been raised over time and were documented in 1990.

The library binding industry, when faced with change or an attack on established practices, chose to view the intense scrutiny of its products as an incentive to conduct research, answer questions, and explore options for technical development. Rigorous testing carried out following the publication of the 1990 edition of the *Guide* resulted in the general adoption of new practices, the superiority of which we now have evidence. Today it can be said that the binding industry has nearly universally addressed the issues documented in 1990.

For example, in 1991 the first modern in-line machine for manufacturing notched, double-fan adhesive bindings was introduced by the library binding industry. The machine mills, notches, double-fan glues, and lines the spines of text blocks of many sizes. This was just the beginning of a series of important advances in equipment and materials. Robotic stamping became viable with the introduction of an acrylic-coated, polyester/cotton blend fabric. This improved material—thinner, flatter, and free of knots—also facilitated automated cover making. Because LBI took the initiative to test and approve new materials, processes that were not feasible in the first decades of the library binding industry have become routine.

In short, the *Guide* documented a well-established need for better and more diverse binding products. The binding industry responded with advances in technology that made those products possible and affordable. Subsequently, the trade association-sponsored *LBI Standard* was overhauled and recast as a performance-based standard, *ANSI/NISO/LBI Z39.78-2000, Library Binding Standard.* This significant shift in approach allows for improvements in methods and materials provided that performance is equaled or exceeded. It is heartening to realize that the years of discussion and discovery among librarians, library binders, and suppliers paved the way for major changes in the field, all of which have benefited and supported the goals of libraries and readers.

Jan Merrill-Oldham

Paul Parisi

July 2008

Reference Notes

1. Jan Merrill-Oldham and Paul Parisi, *Guide to the Library Binding Institute Standard for Library Binding* (Chicago: ALA, 1990); Jan Merrill-Oldham and Paul Parisi, *Library Binding Institute Standard for Library Binding,* 8th ed. (Rochester, N.Y.: The Institute, 1986).
2. ANSI/NISO/LBI, *ANSI/NISO/LBI Z39.78-2000 Library Binding Standard* (Bethesda, Md.: NISO Press, 2000).

Preface to the 1990 edition

In 1986, the eighth edition of the *Library Binding Institute Standard for Library Binding* (referred to herein as the *LBI Standard*) was published by the Library Binding Institute, a trade association of commercial library binders established in 1935. A growing interest among librarians in commercial library binding technology, fueled by the increased attention being paid to the preservation of library collections, resulted in widespread distribution of the new *Standard*. That document, however, consists of technical specifications developed for industry use. Because the *LBI Standard* is written based on the assumption that the reader understands the machinery and processes employed by the library binding industry, descriptive text is minimal. Where treatment options are available and this is often the case, there is no discussion of the advantages and disadvantages of each, or how to choose the most appropriate option in a given situation.

A *Guide to the Library Binding Institute Standard for Library Binding* is a supplement and complement to the *LBI Standard*. While the *Guide* does not repeat the text of the *LBI Standard* its numbering scheme parallels the *LBI Standard* to facilitate side-by-side reading of the two documents. The *Guide* represents an attempt to translate technical jargon into language that can be readily understood by the librarian, and was written with the hope that enhanced technical knowledge will enable librarians to use the *LBI Standard* to its fullest advantage. Procedures are described in greater detail in the *Guide* than in the *LBI Standard*. Where treatment options are listed in the *LBI Standard*, the *Guide* provides evaluative information that assists the librarian in making decisions. The *Guide* presents an historical context, discusses research and development issues, and acknowledges unresolved controversy.

Since the purpose of the *Guide* is to clarify its parent document and to improve communication between librarians and binders, use of terminology has been strictly limited so that terms correspond to those found in the *LBI Standard* and no analogous terms are substituted. The word "endpaper" is used exclusively for example—not interchangeably with "endsheet" or "endleaf." Regarding illustrations, they rarely stand alone. They are meant to help readers understand better what they are seeing as they study the features of a bound volume. The appendixes are a series of management and training tools.

The initiators of this project were the members of the former Library/Binders Relations Committee (now the Physical Quality and Treatment Committee) of the Preservation of Library Materials Section (PLMS), Association for Library Collections and Technical Services, a division of the American Library Association. For those who wonder why PLMS deemed the effort worthwhile, we credit the changing times in American libraries. All editions of the *LBI Standard* previous to 1986 were predicated on the prevailing opinion that the following steps invariably yield a superior binding: milling the spine of a volume to remove spine lining, glue, and thread; oversewing the resulting loose leaves together; trimming the fore edge, head, and tail of the sewn text block; rounding and backing the text block; and fitting it into a pyroxylin-impregnated, buckram-covered case with ⅛" wide squares at the fore edge, head, and tail.

Today, any one (or all) of the procedures cited above may be changed or eliminated, depending upon the binding situation at hand. This departure from tradition has occurred because our criteria for evaluating a successful binding have changed. Librarians are looking beyond sturdiness to user-friendly volumes that can be read and photocopied easily. They recognize that different volumes may require different treatments in order to achieve the combined qualities of durability and openability. As librarians' interest in and expectations of library binding become more complex, so too does library binding itself. We expect that the current evolution within the industry has yet to run its course, and anticipate that this *Guide* will prove to be the first in an ongoing series of interpretive supplements to a maturing industry standard.

The *Guide to the Library Binding Institute Standard for Library Binding* could not have been written without the tremendous support we received from the Library Binding Institute and the community of preservation administrators and library binders who reviewed many, many drafts. Finally, we owe thanks to our advisory committee, which conceived this project, helped to shape and determine the content of the *Guide,* contributed text, and corrected and amended drafts. We hope that the end result will be a useful working tool for those within our profession who share an interest in maintaining and improving the condition of library collections.

Jan Merrill-Oldham

Paul Parisi

June 1990

Commentary on the *Standard*

FOREWORD

The foreword to the *ANSI/NISO/LBI Z39.78-2000, Library Binding Standard* defines the principal mission of the library binding industry as extending "the useful life of library books and periodicals."

The reference to library books and periodicals might be better phrased:

> the useful life of worn and damaged hardcover books as well as periodicals, paperback books, pamphlets, music scores and parts, dissertations and theses, spiral- and comb-bound leaves, and other printed materials that benefit from the protection of hard covers.

Commentary on the *Standard*

INTRODUCTION

1. Purpose and Scope

The stated scope of the *ANSI/NISO/LBI Z39.78-2000, Library Binding Standard*, hereafter cited as the *Standard*, should be interpreted broadly. As noted in the foreword, "books" refers to many types of printed materials.

The descriptions of volume types, methods, and materials laid out in the *Standard* reduce the need for item-by-item binding instructions. By referencing the specifications in the *Standard* and related recommendations in this *Guide*, binding instructions can be provided by category (in case x, do thus), shifting much of the burden of decision making from library to binder.

The binding referred to throughout this document is the product of the commercial library binding industry. Once a part of the Book Manufacturing Institute, library binders established independence in 1935, founding their own trade association. Active continuously since that time, the Library Binding Institute (LBI) promotes excellence and efficiency in the binding and rebinding of library materials. The nature of library binding is best portrayed by comparing its processes and products to publishers' binding. Two factors account for significant differences.

First is the nature of the raw material. When a newly printed book is received by a publishers' binder, each copy (there may be tens of thousands of identical copies printed) is the same size and shape, and is in mint condition. Publishers' binders can take advantage of this uniformity, using high-speed automated equipment for most binding operations. A single, modern production line operated by as few as ten people can bind as many as 3,600 hard-cover books per hour. In contrast, the volumes that are processed by the library binder vary in structure and condition, and require widely varying treatments. Decisions must be made at many stages of production and a complex mixture of machine and hand processes is employed. A library bindery staffed by 30 people might produce 75 volumes per hour, although output varies considerably across the industry depending upon a company's product mix and the extent to which it has automated processes. Calculating very roughly, however, the difference in time required for publishers' vs. library binding is 144 volumes to 1. (If this discussion seems to contradict earlier comments about advances in library binding automation, it is because the differences that separates hand, library, and publishers' binding are considerable. Library binding can come closer to the higher production levels of publishers' binding, but can in no way bridge the gap.)

Second is the orientation of the bindery. The chief concerns of most book publishers are the speed and cost of manufacture, and the appearance of the volume, e.g., the appeal of the cover and jacket design. The quality of the materials used, including adhesives, thread, board, and covering material, is not a primary consideration. Rather, materials must be inexpensive and compatible with high-speed machinery. In contrast, the goal of the library binder is to produce a volume that is sturdy, durable, and flexible. To achieve this goal, library binders use high-quality materials, employ a range of binding techniques, and frequently perform semicustom hand work. Durability is paramount; aesthetic considerations are secondary.

1.1 Books

"First-time hardcover binding of paperbound books for library use" refers to the hardcover binding of paperback books, pamphlets, music scores and parts, dissertations and theses, spiral- and comb-bound leaves, and other printed materials that meet the criteria for books as described in Section 5.1 of the *Standard.*

"Rebinding of hard cover books" refers to the rebinding of any volume that is already hard bound and that has become worn or damaged.

"First-time hardcover binding of paperbound books for library use" and "rebinding of hardcover books" is sometimes referred to as prebinding. Prebound books are manufactured and sold to libraries as a more durable product than publishers' hardbound books. Prebound volumes may or may not meet the specifications of the *Standard.*

1.2 Periodicals

"First-time hard cover binding of paper-covered serial issues" is the binding of one or more softcover issues of a serial publication into a single hardcover volume.

"Rebinding of hardcover serial volumes for library use" is the rebinding of serial issues that have already been hard bound. This may be required either because the original binding has become worn or damaged, or because issues or a large number of leaves (e.g., indexes, supplements, or replacement pages) must be added, removed, or repositioned in a volume.

1.3 Exceptions

This section recognizes that library binding reduces the artifactual value of a volume, i.e., its value as an object as opposed to its value for the information it conveys. Volumes that have significant artifactual value (e.g., private press books, early or fine printings, first and limited editions of important literary works, books in which authors have made notes) should not be library bound. Repairs should be made by a qualified conservator, and storage in a protective enclosure should be considered, e.g., a paper or board wrapper, corrugated storage container, phase box, or double-tray box. See appendix D.

Certain volumes are different from most serials inasmuch as their individual parts should not be bound together, but rather, must be treated as separate pieces. Music scores with parts are an example.

Volumes that cannot be bound because of their physical characteristics include those that are unusually formatted (e.g., sets of loose plates or maps) and those with very brittle leaves. Storage in a protective enclosure is often an appropriate treatment for unusually formatted volumes. Options for dealing with brittle volumes include digitizing and then printing and binding the work or making it available online, microfilming, replacing the volume with a commercially available reprint (be it paper, film, or a digital version), conservation treatment, and storage in a protective enclosure. The option chosen will depend upon the nature of the publication, the collection development and preservation policies that are in place in the library, and the resources that are available to carry out those policies.

Determining when paper is too brittle to bind is not as straightforward an issue as was once suggested. An embrittled but intact text block, if recased, can often sustain many additional readings provided that it is handled carefully. A volume that is too brittle to bind can usually be identified by noting crumbling page edges; or breaks, fractures, or cracks in the pages, especially near the binding margin. It is important to distinguish simple tears caused by rough handling from paper damage resulting from embrittlement.

Darkened paper sometimes indicates loss of strength, but it is an inadequate indicator. Yellowed paper can be flexible and white paper quite brittle. A reasonable practice is to send questionable volumes to the binder with instructions to recase if possible. These volumes should be flagged in the library's binding records so that they can be inspected carefully when they are returned by the bindery. Study those that have been bound, as well as those marked "too brittle to bind," and learn from each item reviewed. Your decision making will improve with increasing knowledge and practice.

2. Title & Citation

When writing contracts or similar agreements, the title *ANSI/NISO/LBI Z39.78-2000, Library Binding Standard* can be abbreviated to *ANSI/NISO/LBI Standard.* Such terms as "Class A Binding" and "Class B Binding," commonly used in the mid-twentieth century, have become obsolete and should not be used.

3. Representation & Warranty

Most binders whose products adhere to the specifications of the *Standard* also offer products that are not included in the *Standard,* e.g., economy binding, pamphlet binding, and construction of protective enclosures. Furthermore, a bindery need not be a member of the Library Binding Institute to comply with the *Standard.* For more information on supplementary services offered by library binders, see appendixes C and D.

Many binders self-insure customer property and will pay reasonable repair or replacement costs if a volume is damaged or lost. The librarian and the binder must agree upon a repair/replacement value beyond which supplementary insurance is required, and whether there will be a surcharge for that insurance.

4. Compliance

The *Standard* is performance based. The compliance section of the document describes the procedure to be followed when methods or materials outside the scope of the *Standard* will be used. Alternatives must meet or exceed the performance achieved using the methods and materials that are currently specified. Binders who adhere to the *Standard* are by definition in compliance with the *Standard.* Those who wish to innovate must follow a clearly defined testing protocol to validate proposed alternatives. It is hoped that this flexibility will encourage constant improvement.

5. Classification of Volumes

For the purposes of billing, the classification of volumes as books or periodicals is determined by whether reference must be made either to:

a) another physical volume in a set or series, or

b) a binding record that is kept on file by the binder.

There is a cost factor associated with periodicals (in some binderies these include serials and monographic sets and series) because of the need to match type style, placement of spine lettering, and color of covering material. The classification scheme does not refer to the method of binding that will be used nor to its relative strength or quality.

5.1 Book (Monograph)

Books are volumes that can be bound without reference to any other volume. Typically they are single-volume monographs. The lettering stamped on the spine need not be made to match the placement or type size of the lettering on any other volume. Usually the color of covering material is selected by the binder and there is an extra charge levied when the customer makes the selection instead. This is to compensate for the additional time required to pull a particular color, and the added potential for error.

5.2 Periodical (Serial)

Periodicals are generally volumes made up of one or more issues of a serial publication. Usually the issues are of like size. A database of binding patterns is maintained by the binder to ensure to the greatest extent possible that uniform spine lettering, and consistent color of covering material and stamping foil, are maintained from volume to volume despite their not being bound all at once. It is important to be aware that unless the height and thickness of each text block within a title is the same, the point size and orientation of lettering may inevitably vary from volume to volume.

Commentary on the *Standard*

TECHNICAL SPECIFICATIONS

6. Examination, Collation, and Preparation

The following decisions must be made during examination and collation: the method of leaf attachment to be used, whether the edges of the text block will be trimmed, and whether the condition of the text block is such that the volume should not be bound (e.g., because it has brittle paper or missing leaves). These decisions are governed by library policy, which can be communicated to the binder in one of several ways:

a) The library may examine each volume prior to binding and prepare item-specific instructions.

b) The library may provide the binder with general guidelines for making decisions. See appendixes E and F.

c) The library may leave decision making entirely up to the bindery. In this case, it is imperative that the library first assess the binder's standard operating procedures to verify that they are compatible with the library's binding policy.

Regarding selection of an appropriate method of leaf attachment, only oversewing and side sewing require a substantial minimum binding margin. Recasing and sewing through the fold require none, and double-fan adhesive binding requires very little. If these latter three are the primary methods of leaf attachment employed, width of binding margin ceases to be a major concern. For an extended discussion of leaf attachment, see Sections 7.0 through 7.5.2.1 of this *Guide.*

Regarding the condition of the text block, the library should assume responsibility for screening volumes for embrittlement if possible, and remove from the bindery work flow all volumes that are deemed too brittle to bind. In this way the binder will neither run the risk of damaging brittle paper nor expend resources needlessly in returning them to the library unbound. It may take time to learn to recognize books that are outside the scope of the binder's services. See Section 1.3 of this *Guide.*

6.1 Books

While earlier editions of what has become the *Standard* specified page-by-page examination of volumes for completeness and/or correct order of leaves, from 1986 forward the *Standard* omits the requirement for page-by-page inspection, recognizing that this level of attention is extremely expensive. The bindery worker does conduct a cursory examination, but it would be prohibitively expensive for that inspection to be done carefully enough to guarantee that every missing leaf and all leaves out of sequence will be noticed.

Where books have multiple parts (e.g., music scores with parts), the number of parts should be noted in binding instructions.

In the event that the library chooses to bind an incomplete or otherwise defective volume, binding instructions should read, "bind as is."

6.2 Custom Periodicals

No commentary for Section 6.2.

6.3 Standard Periodicals

As in book collation, the binder cannot guarantee that every missing leaf and all leaves out of sequence will be noticed when periodicals are collated. The main differences between custom and standard periodical collation are these: In custom periodical collation the binder removes covers and unpaginated advertisements at the front and back of each issue and repositions the title page, contents, index, and/or supplements as requested by the library. In standard periodical collation the library assumes these tasks if they are to be performed at all. The binder checks only for "completeness and correct order of issues." Binders typically refer to standard periodical collation as, "bind as is."

In making decisions regarding collation, the library must consider such factors as the per-volume cost of binding and the staff time available for in-house bindery preparation. The more preparation work the binder is required to do, the more expensive the overall cost of binding will be. Custom periodical collation is more costly than standard periodical collation, and additional surcharges are levied for removing ads that appear throughout the text (as opposed to those that are grouped at the front and back of the text of each issue). Most libraries choose standard periodical collation. When the library opts to remove advertisements and reposition leaves, however, the binder should be consulted to ensure that this preparation does not preclude desirable binding options. When single leaves are removed from a serial volume made up of signatures, for example, the volume can no longer be sewn through the fold.

The decision to retain the covers of serial issues is problematic. From a bibliographic standpoint, covers often contain important information that cannot be discarded. They also serve as a visual clue, separating weeks, months, or years. The retention of extremely stiff covers, however, can make a volume difficult to handle and read. Stiff covers prevent the leaves of the text block from opening freely and, in the case of adhesive-bound volumes, they strain the adhesive bond. Where covers are extremely stiff, they can be replaced with good photocopies made on alkaline paper. Use of dark cream-colored alkaline sheets can help to retain visual recognition of the spot where one issue stops and another begins. Custom handling such as this is very time consuming and therefore is costly.

6.4 Repair

The transparent pressure-sensitive alkaline paper mending tape that is specified in the *Standard* is available from a variety of library supply houses. It is sometimes referred to as archival mending tape. While it does not, in fact, meet all of the requirements that are implied by the term "archival," it does have advantages over household-type tapes. It is thinner and more flexible, resulting in a less stiff, less noticeable mend, and is easier to remove if necessary. But some formulations may occasionally cause unstable inks to bleed, and rarely, adhesive may creep out from under the edges of the paper carrier and adhere to facing leaves. Superior alternatives include mending with heat-set tissue or with Japanese paper and starch paste. Such archival repairs take time to execute and it is unrealistic to assume that they can be made by library binders. If mending with Japanese paper is desired, the mending should be done by trained personnel in the library before volumes are sent out for binding. Additionally, the binder should be instructed to flag—not mend—torn leaves that were overlooked by the library or were inadvertently damaged at the bindery.

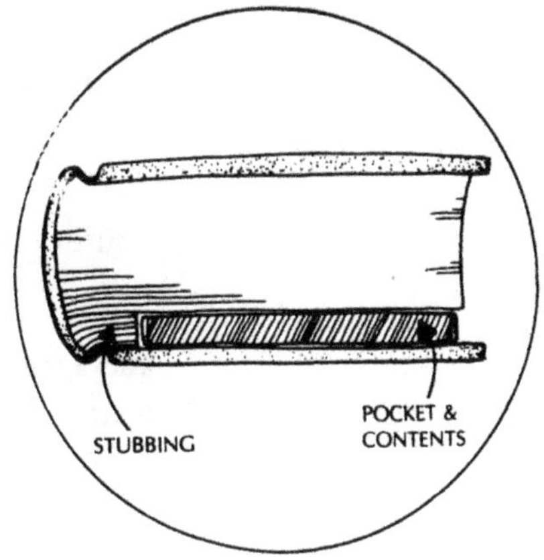

Figure 1. Stubbing

This is not to say that binders are incapable of making archival-quality paper repairs, because some are; but archival mending is an expensive commercial service for routine applications. It requires time and space for working and drying, and moves a volume off-line. Mending policies should be spelled out clearly in binding contracts.

6.5 Maps, Illustrations, and Folded Leaves

When a volume contains folded maps, charts, or other folded leaves, special care must be taken to ensure that they are not damaged by spine milling, oversewing, side sewing, or trimming. Folded leaves, for example, can be accidentally cut during spine milling. To prevent this, volumes with folded leaves should be recased or sewn through the fold if possible—methods that do not require milling. If neither option is possible, the volume should be double-fan adhesive bound. Oversewing and side sewing require the use of more binding margin, and there is a chance that sewing thread will pass through the fore edge of a folded leaf and prevent it from opening. Volumes with folded leaves should be left untrimmed to ensure that folds at the fore edge, head, and/or tail are not cut away. Alternatively, maps can be refolded and set out on hinges to prevent damage to folds during binding, but this is an expensive process best carried out at the library, and the results are often unsatisfactory.

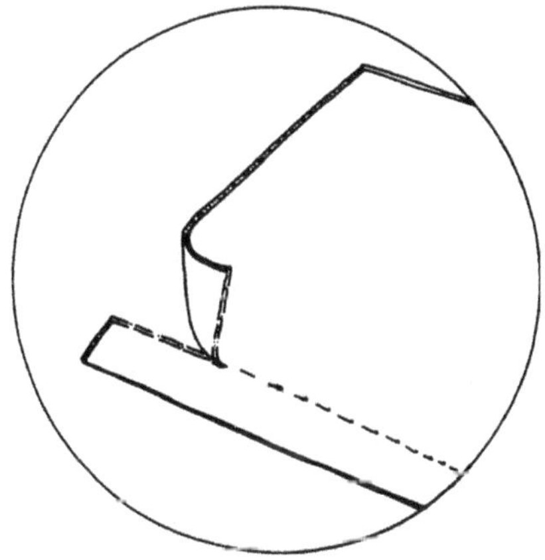

Figure 2. Single perforated sheet bound in with others to create stubbing.

In some cases the best treatment for folded leaves is to separate them from the text and house them separately in a pocket attached to the inside of the back cover of the bound volume. If the resulting insert will cause the book to be significantly thicker at the fore edge than at the spine, stubbing must be added to the text block before binding so that the spine of the case is wide enough to accommodate the pocket. See figure 1.

Stubbing is made by binding perforated paper in with the text block. After the volume is bound, the blank leaves are torn away along their perforations, leaving ½"-wide stubs. These create space for a pocket and insert. See figure 2. It must be noted that while stubbing makes it possible to house loose material together with a bound text, it forms a stiff ridge over which leaves must flex, thus interfering with openability. See figure 3. Furthermore, aging leaves can break against the hard edges of the stubbing, particularly as paper loses its strength. Where openability is particularly important, as in the case of music

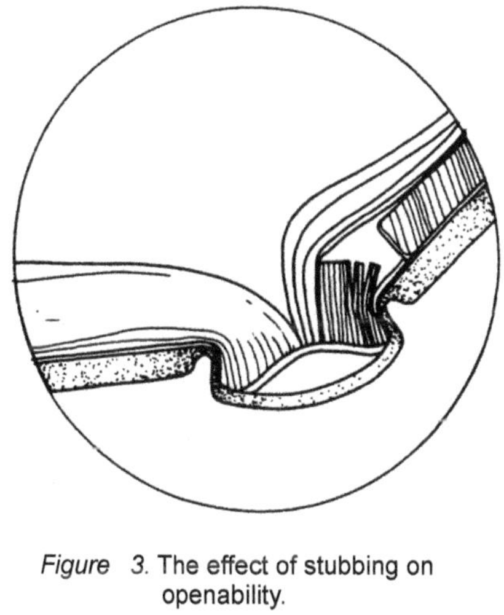

Figure 3. The effect of stubbing on openability.

scores, this option should not be used. An alternative treatment is to catalog thick packets of unbindable material separately and house them in a protective enclosure.

Music scores and accompanying parts require special treatment. An ideal approach is to bind the score, sew each part into its own paper or paper-lined limp buckram cover, and house the score and all the bound parts together in a protective enclosure.

The library should discuss the issues covered in this section of the *Guide* with the binder and agree upon approaches to treatment. As extra insurance against error, specific binding instructions should be provided for each volume that has folded leaves, loose leaves, or separate parts.

7. Attaching the Leaves

"Attaching the leaves" refers to the process by which the leaves of a text block are joined together with sewing thread or adhesive. There are five methods of leaf attachment described in the *Standard.* They appear in order of preference, and their descriptions are followed by sections on:

1) preparation,
2) attaching endpapers, and
3) endpaper construction.

This *Guide* includes an additional section under each method of leaf attachment describing its advantages and disadvantages.

4a. Paper grain runs perpendicular to bound edge.

4b. Paper grain runs parallel to bound edge.

Figure 4. Effect of grain direction on openability.

Prior to 1986, the *Standard* emphasized oversewing nearly to the exclusion of all other methods of leaf attachment. It is now recognized that other options are typically preferable. The narrow binding margins in many publications, coupled with widespread use of photocopy machines and scanners in libraries, argue for preserving as much as possible of the binding margin and using binding methods that do not restrict openability. Recasing, sewing through the fold, and double-fan adhesive binding all result in volumes that open to the very inner edge of each leaf and lie as flat as possible, given the grain direction of the paper. See discussion in Sections 7.2.2.2 and 7.4.2.1.

By way of example, texts that must be consulted while the reader's hands are otherwise engaged (as in reading printed music or a cook book) must lie very flat. The best way to achieve this functionality is to recase already-sewn text blocks or to sew loose signatures through the fold. Where the text block is made up of single sheets rather than folded signatures, double-fan adhesive binding is the next best option. This is true for all books, but since sewing through the fold is more expensive than adhesive binding, it might be specified only for those categories of material where maximum openability is imperative.

Oversewing would rarely be appropriate for books that must lie flat, e.g., music scores. See figures 4 and 5. Information about each method can be found in Sections 7.1 through 7.5.2.1 of this *Guide*, in the many articles on the topic that appear in past issues of *Shelf Life* (a periodical published by LBI), and by visiting one or more library binderies. Once the technology is understood, criteria for making decisions should be agreed upon and incorporated into the customer profile. A decision tree can facilitate selection by the library or bindery of appropriate methods of leaf attachment. See appendix A.

7.1 Recasing

There are two questions to consider when determining whether a text block can be recased:

- Is the text block sewn through the fold, side-sewn, or oversewn (rather than adhesive bound)?

  The answer must be yes.

- Is the sewing structure in good condition, with the possible exception of loose first and last signatures?

  The answer must be yes.

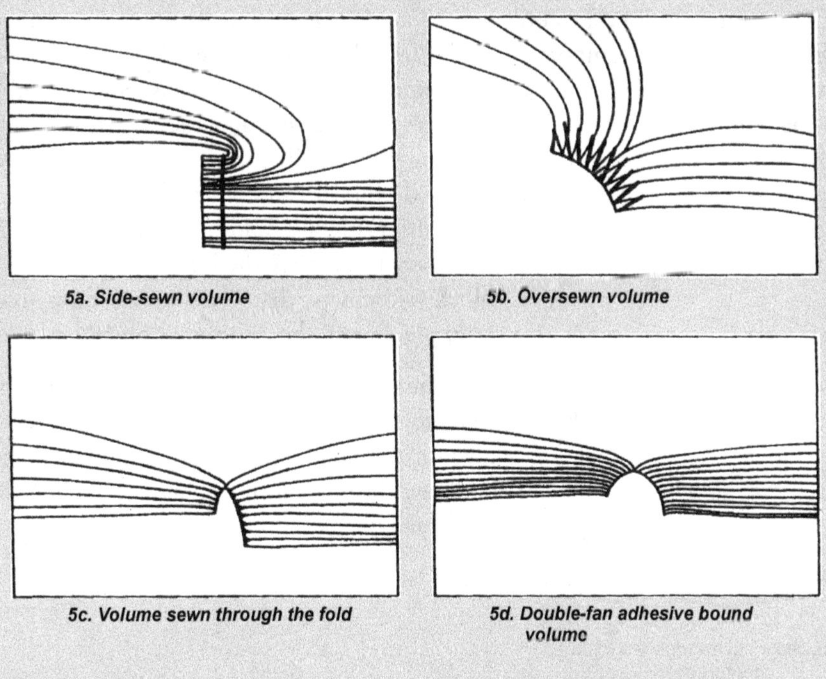

Figure 5. Comparing openability among methods of leaf attachment used in library binding.

Note that to call recasing a method of leaf attachment is misleading. The treatment actually involves replacing the original case with a new one without altering the existing leaf attachment. The text block is removed from its original case, old lining material and adhesive are removed from the spine if possible, new endpapers are attached, the spine is coated with adhesive, a strong spine lining is applied, a new case is made, and the case is attached to the text block.

Recasing is an appropriate treatment for any volume that has a sewn text block in good condition. Many new paperbacks and worn and damaged monographs fall into this category, as do music scores and parts, and hard-bound serial volumes with worn and damaged covers.

While an adhesive-bound text block *can* be recased, double-fan adhesive binding is the preferred option unless binding margins are so narrow that milling is undesirable. The hot melt adhesives used by publishers' binders sometimes fail, particularly in older volumes, and are sometimes hard and stiff, inhibiting openability. The cold emulsion adhesives used by library binders have proven to be long-lasting and flexible, and the double-fan method results in secure leaf attachment.

Care must be taken when inspecting a volume before recasing to determine whether the text block is sewn. Turn to the centermost fold of a signature and locate the sewing thread. Some methods used by publishers' binders involve piercing slots through the folds of signatures and forcing adhesive (usually hot melt adhesive) into these slots. See figure 6. The result is a volume with signatures still intact, but held together by adhesive rather than thread. "Burst bindings" can be recased to avoid milling and to preserve signatures, but check carefully to be sure that the pages are attached securely.

For volumes that are sewn through the fold, the condition of the original sewing must be assessed after the text block has been removed from its case. Look closely at the sewing thread. If it is unbroken or broken only at the first and last signatures, it can be repaired and the text block recased. It is important not to mistake gaps between signatures for broken sewing thread. Gaps and wobbliness will be remedied when the spine is re-glued and lined. If the sewing thread is broken anywhere other than the first and last signatures, however, options narrow. The sewing can be repaired or replaced, but because these treatments are time consuming, they should be considered only if it is necessary to preserve the folds of signatures. A text block with maps that bleed across folds may, for example, have to be repaired or resewn.

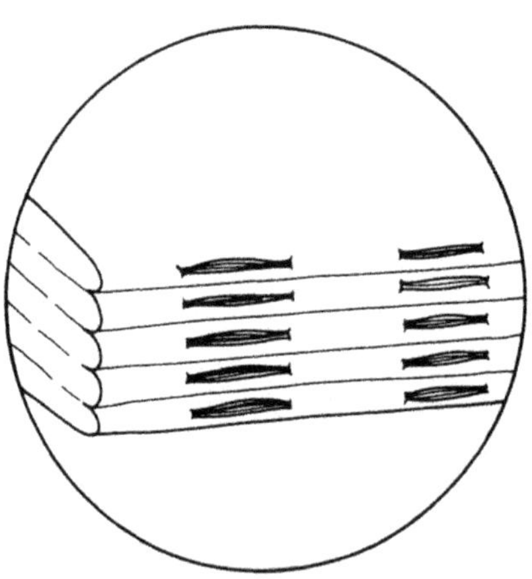

Figure 6. Slots cut through the folds of signatures.

The library and the binder should discuss the steps to be taken when the bindery discovers that a volume earmarked for recasing cannot be bound this way. The resulting policy should be incorporated into the customer profile. See appendix F.

7.1.1 Preparation

In the days when the spines of most publishers' bindings were consolidated with animal glue, all of the old spine lining material and as much as possible of the old adhesive could be removed in preparation for recasing, exercising caution to avoid breaking the sewing thread.

Today book manufacturers use hot melt, polyurethane, and rarely, polyvinyl acetate adhesives to consolidate the leaves of text blocks. These adhesives cannot be removed using any reasonable technique. Most hot melts, for example, are wax based (not water based) and their running temperature can be as high as 350 °F. Heating to remove them is not an option. Fortunately, it is unnecessary to remove modern adhesives from sewn text blocks before recasing, since they will retain their adhesive properties over time.

7.1.2 Attaching the Endpapers

While the *Standard* specifies that for text blocks that are sewn through the fold, endpapers shall be sewn on through the fold, some binders tip endpapers on instead, particularly where small and medium-sized volumes are concerned. Sewing has the advantage of anchoring endpapers to the text block securely but it is more expensive than tipping on. Techniques that restrict openability of the volume should be avoided.

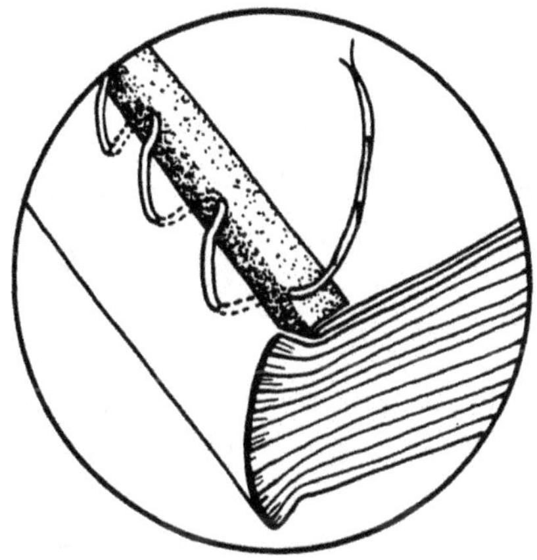

Figure 7. Whip stitching.*

The method most commonly used before the introduction of the 1986 edition of the *Standard* was whip stitching. This involves overcasting an oversew-style endpaper to the front and back of the text block using five to seven widely spaced stitches. See figure 7. Whip stitching prevents the first and last sections of the text block from opening fully, thus diminishing the benefit of recasing. Furthermore, the folded-back oversew-style endpaper creates a sharp edge along which aging paper can break. See figure 8.

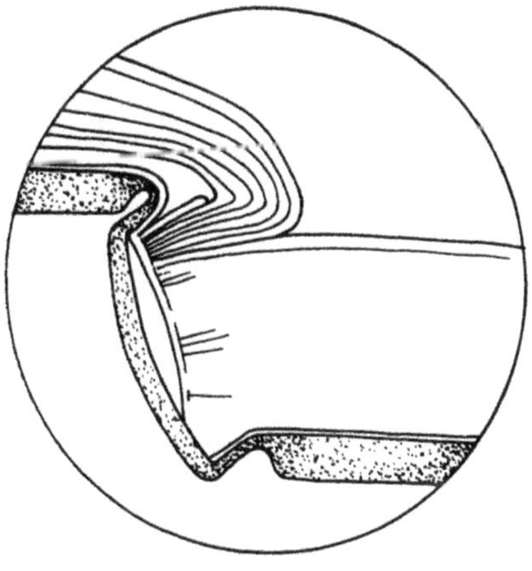

Figure 8. Restricted openability resulting from whip stitching.

Whip stitching is acceptable for attaching endpapers to oversewn or side-sewn volumes that are being recased, since no other means of attaching endpapers is practical and openability is already restricted by the sewing structure.

The library should be aware of the method that is being used by the binder to attach endpapers to recased text blocks and should make a point of observing that process when visiting the bindery.

7.1.2.1 Endpaper Construction

All three of the endpapers used for sewing multiple-signature text blocks through the fold can also be used when text blocks are recased. See Sections 7.2.2.1 and 7.2.2.2 of the *Standard* and this *Guide* and figures 9, 10, and 11.

In addition to these three styles is a fourth: a single folded sheet with a reinforcing hinge that extends beyond the fold. See figure 12. The extension may be left to hinge freely between the endpaper and the text block, or can be glued to the spine of the text block. The free hinge improves the appearance and functioning of the bound volume at the junction between the endpapers and text block.

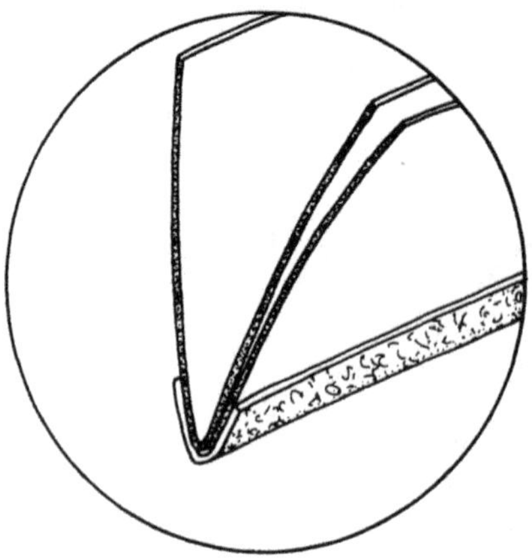

Figure 9. Endpaper for multiple-signature text blocks. Option 1.

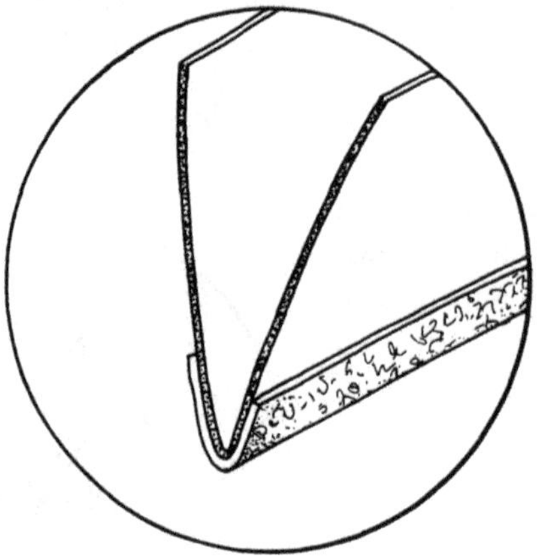

Figure 10. Endpaper for multiple-signature text blocks. Option 2.

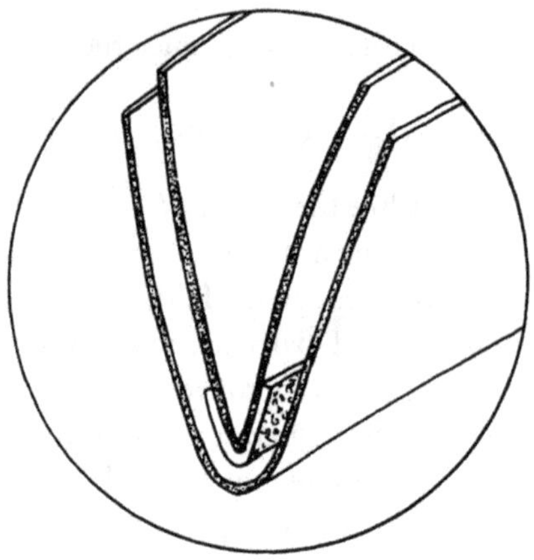

Figure 11. Endpaper for multiple-signature text blocks. Option 3.

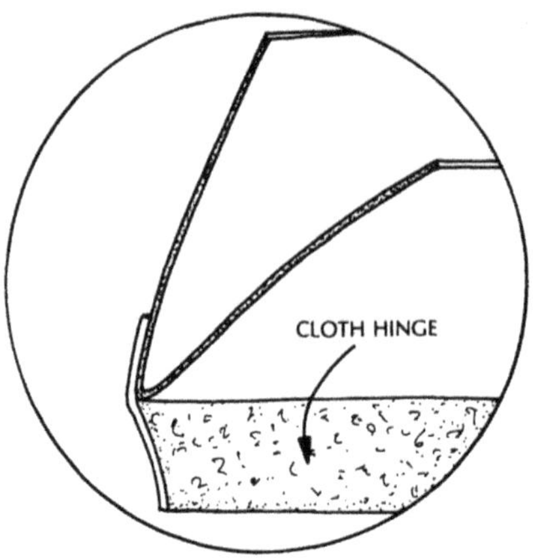

Figure 12. Endpaper for recasing. Option 4.

Advantages of Recasing

- No binding margin has to be milled away in preparation for recasing. The entire binding margin remains intact.
- The text block retains the same degree of openability that it had before it was rebound, or the openability is improved because the stiff original adhesive had been removed from the spine.
- The original sewing structure remains unchanged.

Disadvantages of Recasing

- Recasing is more expensive than double-fan adhesive binding. It can involve removal of the old spine lining and adhesive, sewing new endpapers on through the fold, rounding and backing by hand, in cases where the text block is misshapen, and hand trimming the endpapers (in cases where the text block itself is left untrimmed). See Section 10.0 of this Guide.

7.2 Sewing Through the Fold

There are two questions to consider when determining whether a text block can be sewn through the fold:

- Is the text block made up of one or more signatures?

  The answer must be yes.

- Are the signatures unsewn — that is, are they separate from each other? See figure 13.

  The answer must be yes.

Monographs that have signatures are rarely resewn through the fold by the library binder because it is first necessary to remove all of the old lining material and adhesive from the spine, cut and remove sewing threads, pull signatures apart, and repair damaged folds—a time-consuming and expensive process. There are instances, however, where such custom treatment is necessary. An atlas, for example, may have plates that bleed across two facing pages.

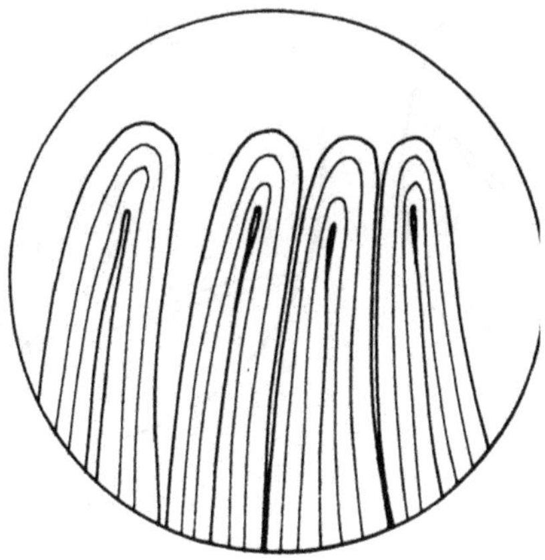

Figure 13. Separate signatures.

Milling away the folds of signatures could result in loss of critical information. When sewing through the fold is the only option that will preserve text and illustrations, and text block preparation can be undertaken by skilled library staff, this work is done most cost-effectively in-house.

Serial issues that are published in single-signature format are the most likely candidates for sewing through the fold. *Time*, *Newsweek*, and single-signature music scores are good examples of this type of publication.

While the decision to sew through the fold can be made by the library, whether that sewing will be done by machine or by hand must be decided at the bindery. The choice is dictated by the limitations of machinery. Signatures can be either too thin or too thick to sew by machine, and paper can be too hard. Machine sewing will be done whenever possible, however, since it is easier and less expensive than hand sewing.

7.2.1 Preparation

All staples must be removed before sewing through the fold because they rust in humid conditions and can erode the paper surrounding them.

While use of pressure-sensitive tape is not the optimal method of repairing damaged paper, it is the only cost-effective method that can be recommended for use by library binders on general library collections. See Section 6.4 of this *Guide* for comments regarding archival paper repair.

Provided they are properly positioned in the text block, loose inserts such as errata slips are automatically sewn into oversewn and side-sewn volumes, and automatically glued into double-fan adhesive-bound volumes. They must, however, be tipped or hinged into volumes that will be sewn through the fold. Binders typically tip in loose leaves because it is the less time-consuming option, and reserve hinging-in for situations where a loose leaf is very stiff and heavy. Hinging-in can be done in several ways, all of which involve adhering a paper hinge to the loose leaf along its binding edge. The hinged leaf can then be sewn through the fold and into the text block, or the hinge of the leaf can be pasted to the binding margin

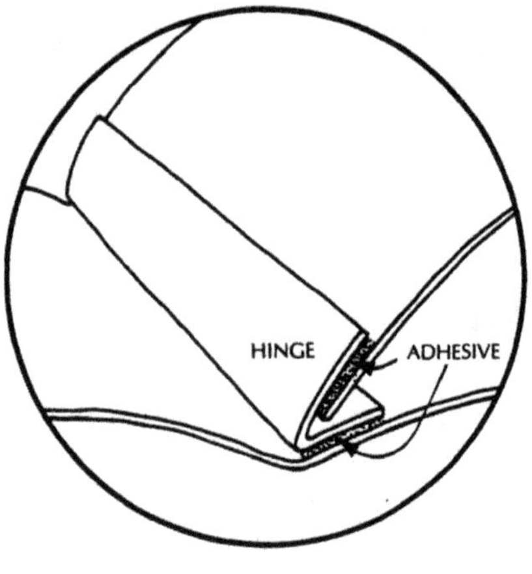

Figure 14. Hinged-in leaf.*

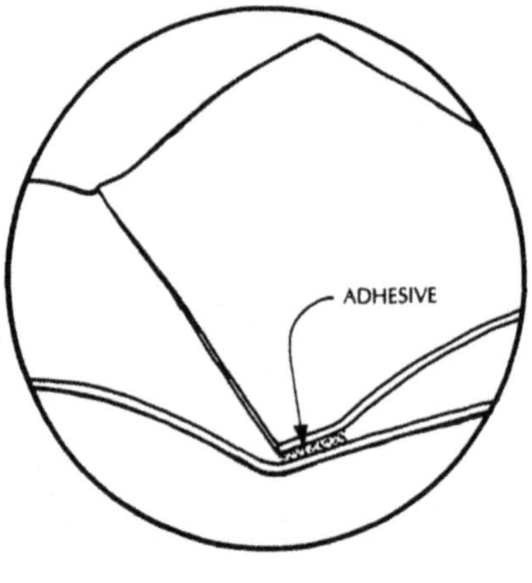

Figure 15. Tipped-in leaf.*

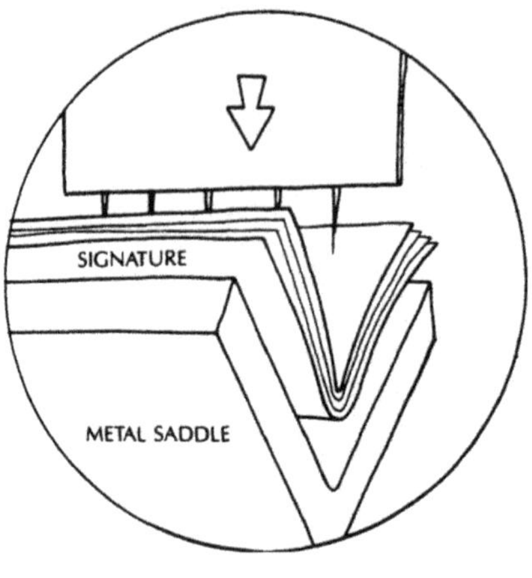

Figure 16. Punching the fold of a signature positioned on a metal saddle.

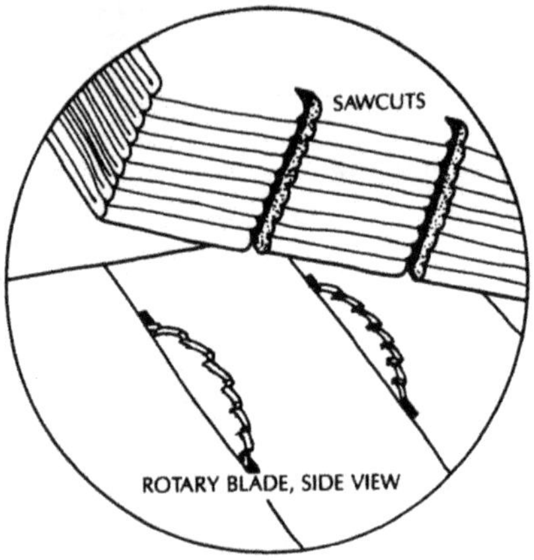

Figure 17. Saw-cutting the spine of a text block to create sewing holes

Figure 18. Rectangular slots, made by a rotary saw along the fold of a signature.

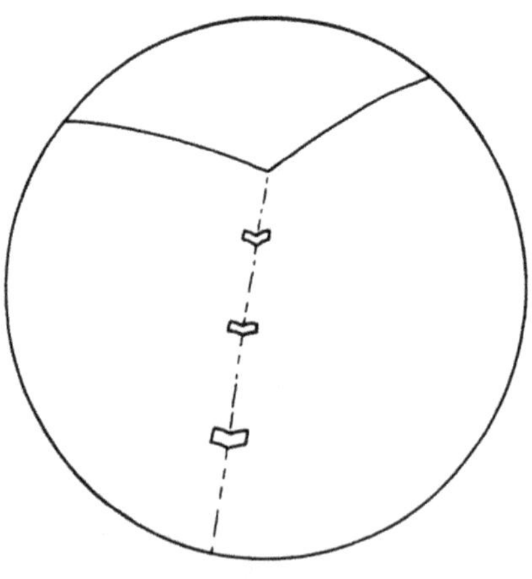

Figure 19. Slots, made by a rotary saw, visible in an open text block.

of a leaf in the text block. See figure 14. Hinging involves far more work than tipping in, but it allows a leaf to turn freely without putting stress on the adjacent pages. See figure 15.

The *Standard* describes two methods for making sewing holes for hand sewing: punching and saw-cutting. Punching is done by placing each signature onto a saddle or into a V-shaped trough, one at a time, and forcing an awl or drill through its fold at intervals; or by piercing the signature once with a multiple-needle perforating device. See figure 16. This can be a labor-intensive process, particularly for volumes with many signatures.

In contrast, saw-cutting is done by jogging all loose signatures together so that they are flush at the spine and tail, and passing the spine of the text block perpendicularly across a rotary saw blade. See figure 17. Successive cuts are made across the spine (from five to seven cuts, depending upon the height of the text block). The sewing holes thus created along the fold of the signature are actually rectangular slots. See figures 18 and 19.

Because it is difficult for the binder to gauge accurately how deeply to make these cuts, the slots almost always extend farther into the binding margin than is necessary. Furthermore, because the slots are sometimes large, excessive adhesive may seep into them during spine lining. While use of a rotary saw is faster than punching sewing holes, and the slots made by the saw are easy to sew through, punched holes are considerably less damaging and result in a more secure sewing structure.

7.2.1.1 Sewing through the Fold by Hand

The hand-sewing process is best understood by watching bindery staff sew a volume and by inspecting the finished product. Two methods of hand sewing are described in the *Standard*—sewing on tapes and sewing on sawn-in cords, but cords are no longer used by library binders. See figures 20 and 21.

Tapes run perpendicularly across the spine of the volume and provide a framework around which the sewing structure is built. Tapes are completely external to the text block, provide strong, gentle support, and do not restrict its openability.

The definition of sewing "all along" that appears in this *Guide* and in the glossary of the *Standard* explains why it is a method superior to sewing two-on.

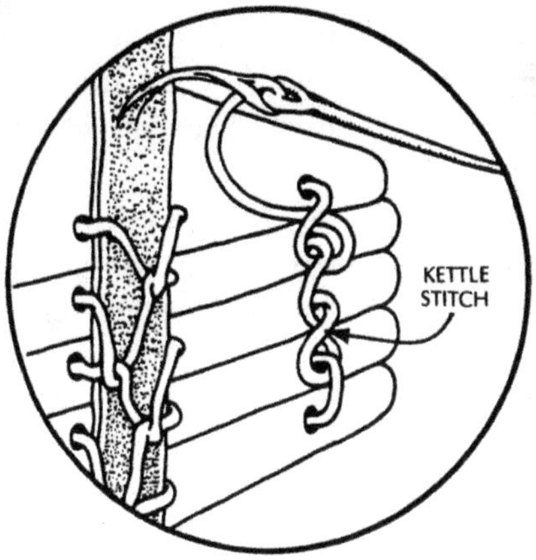

Figure 20. Hand sewing on tapes.*

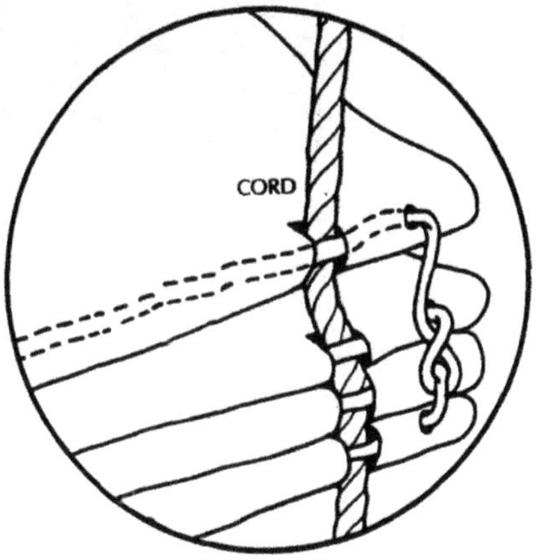

Figure 21. Hand sewing on sawn-in cords.*

Typically, when a text block that consists of only one signature is sewn through the fold by hand, five sewing holes are made along the fold of the signature and it is sewn into endpapers using a figure-eight pattern. See figures 22 and 23. A particularly tall folio, however, may require seven sewing holes. The figure-eight pattern is an excellent sewing structure for single-signature volumes because the long stitches support the text block securely without perforating it excessively.

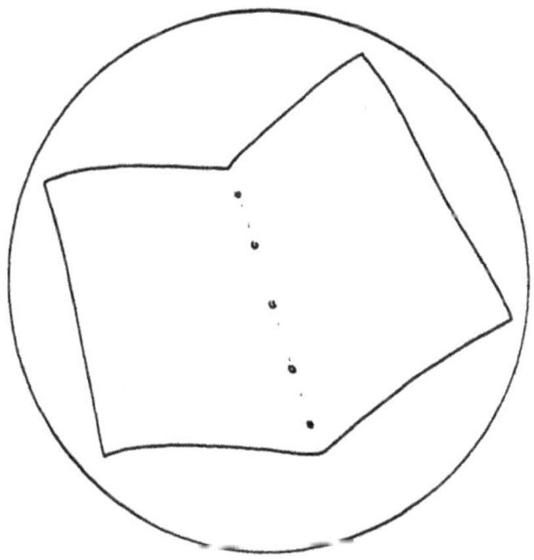
Figure 22. Five holes punched for hand sewing a single signature through the fold.

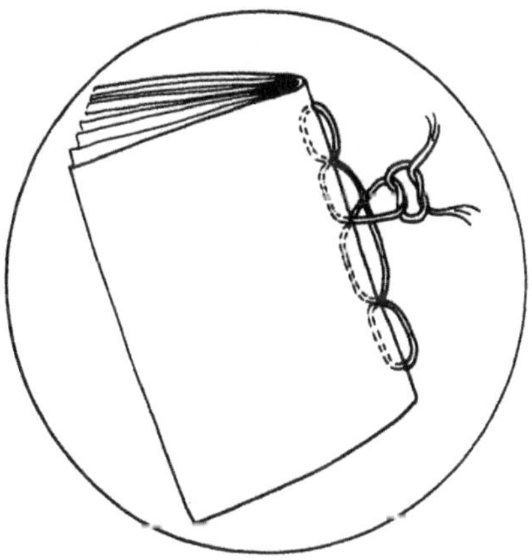
Figure 23. Figure-eight sewing structure.

7.2.1.2 Sewing through the Fold by Machine

For volumes having multiple signatures, machine sewing through the fold is done by library binders on equipment that makes the same type of sewing stitch as the Smyth machines used by publishers' binders. Library binders, however, typically use National or Martini sewing machines, either of which is well suited to sewing volumes of varying size up to 17" tall and 15" wide. Signatures must be hand-fed onto the machine one after another, at a rate of approximately three signatures per minute. In contrast, the Smyth sewing machine can sew as many as 220 signatures per minute, and is designed for high-volume production of large runs of identical books.

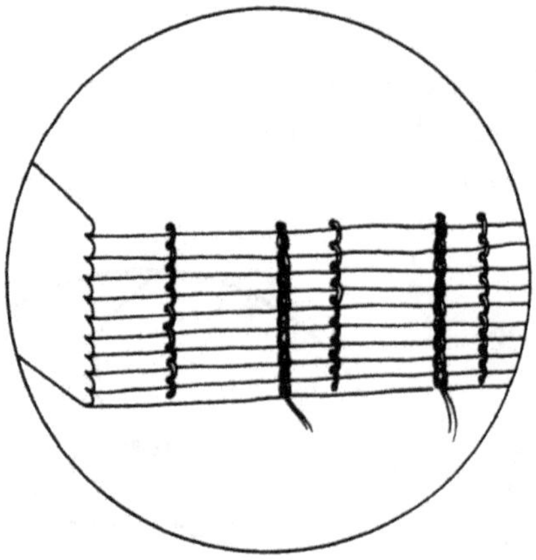

Figure 24. Spine of a machine-sewn text block.

To sew a text block through the fold, the operator places the front endpaper over a metal saddle on the sewing machine. When a foot pedal is depressed, the saddle moves into sewing position. Punches pierce upward through the fold of the endpaper, creating sewing holes. Pairs of sewing needles and hooks pass downward through the punched holes and form stitches that are similar to crochet stitches. See figure 24. After the endpaper is sewn, the metal saddle moves back into feeding position leaving the sewn endpaper at the sewing station. The first signature of the text block is then placed on the saddle, the foot pedal is depressed, the signature moves into position, and the process is repeated. Successive signatures are sewn one to the next and, finally, to the back endpaper. A last depression of the foot pedal locks the stitches.

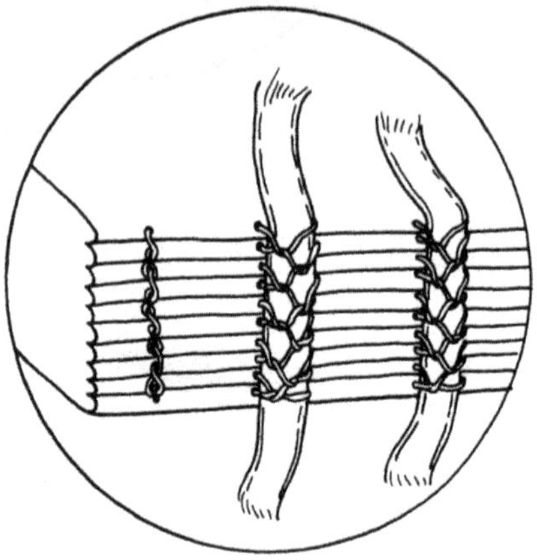

Figure 25. Spine of a hand-sewn text block.

In the past, tapes were sometimes incorporated into volumes sewn-through-the-fold by machine. It is no longer believed that this practice adds enough additional support to justify the extra cost. Whereas tapes are needed in hand sewing to link the signatures perpendicularly across the spine, in machine sewing this linking is accomplished by the sewing threads themselves. See figure 25.

The machine used to sew through the fold of a single-signature volume can best be described as a large version of a household sewing machine, except that it is capable of handling thicker thread, sewing through more paper, and making longer stitches. The sewing process is sometimes called "Singer sewing." Stitches, which run along the fold of the signature, are called lock stitches. See figure 26. They should be at least ½" long—and the longer the better. When sewing holes are too closely spaced, the fold of the signature is weakened by perforations, and as the paper ages it may split along the line of sewing. See figure 27. Contrast this process with sewing a single signature through the fold by hand, which requires only five or seven sewing holes. Find more information in Section 7.2.1.1 of this *Guide.*

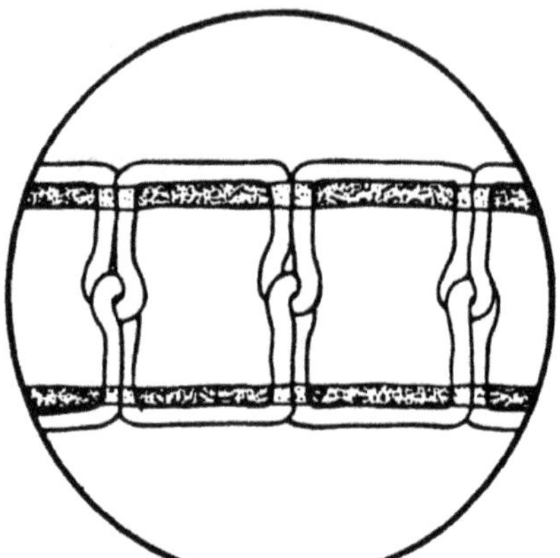

Figure 26. Lock stitch.*

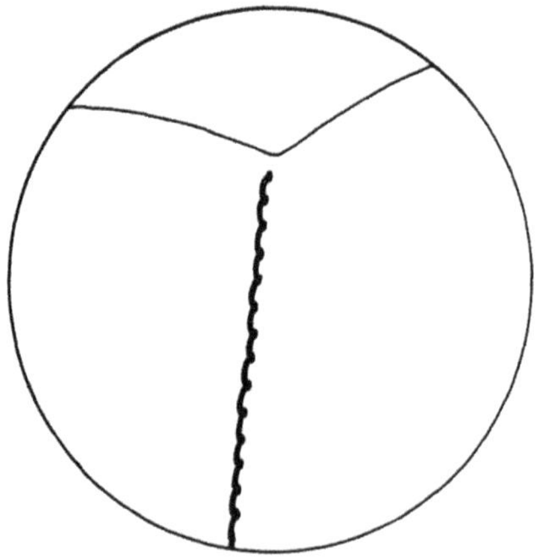

Figure 27. Closely spaced sewing holes made by Singer-type sewing machines.

7.2.2 Attaching Endpapers

No commentary for Section 7.2.2.

7.2.2.1 Endpaper Construction for Text Blocks Comprising Multiple Signatures

There are three styles of endpapers used when sewing multiple-signature text blocks through the fold. In each case a pair of endpapers serves as the first and last signatures of the sewn text block. See figure 28. The three types of endpapers described in the *Standard* appear in figures 9, 10 and 11 of this *Guide.*

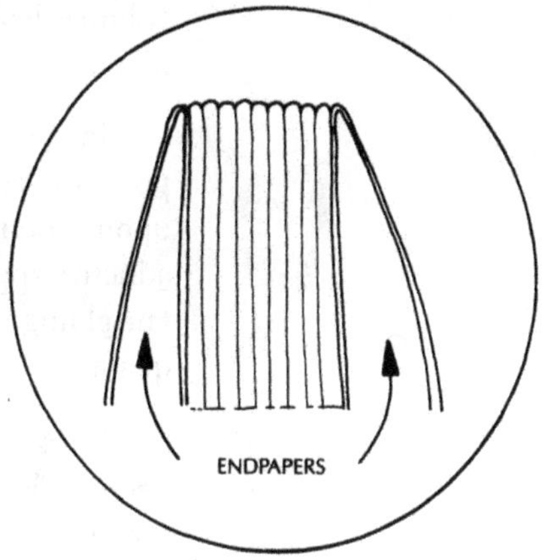

Figure 28. Endpapers at the front and back of a multiple-signature text block.

7.2.2.2 Endpaper Construction for Text Blocks Comprising a Single Signature

See figure 29.

Advantages of Sewing through the Fold

- No binding margin has to be milled away in preparation for sewing through the fold. The entire binding margin remains intact.
- Because signatures are sewn through the fold as opposed to through the side, the text block opens to the innermost edge of each leaf and all text is easily readable. The text block lies as flat as possible, given the grain direction of the paper. See figure 30.
- Very little damage is done to a volume when it is sewn through the fold. If the volume must be rebound for any reason, rebinding can be done relatively successfully.

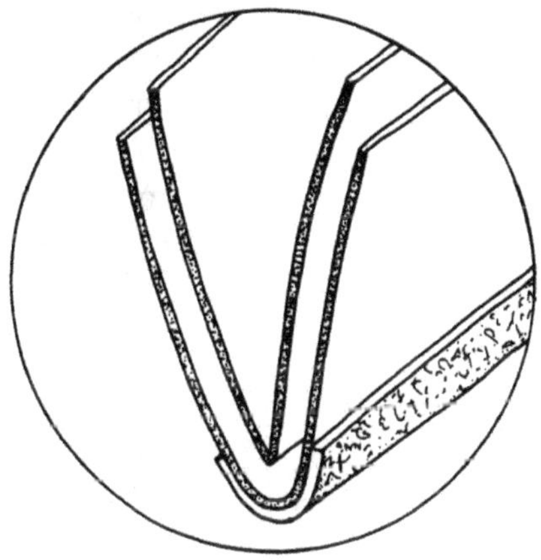

Figure 29. Endpaper for a single signature.

Disadvantage of Sewing through the Fold

- Because preparation of a volume for sewing through the fold, and the sewing itself, takes more time than double-fan adhesive binding, it is more expensive.

7.3 Double-Fan Adhesive Binding

There are three questions to consider when determining whether a text block can be double-fan adhesive bound:

- Can the text block be milled to free the leaves for double-fanning without destroying important text or illustrations?

  The answer must be yes.

- Is the text block 2" thick or less?

  The answer must be yes.

- Is the paper extremely stiff and thick, e.g., plates in architectural books?

  The answer must be no.

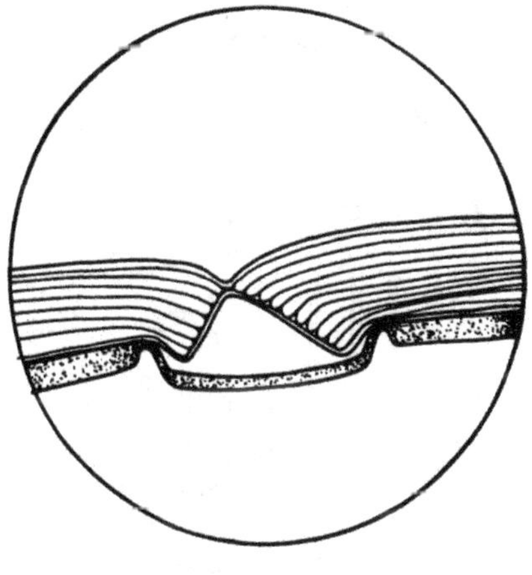

Figure 30. Openability of a text block that is sewn through the fold.

Double-fan adhesive binding was once used in the library binding industry only when volumes had so little binding margin that they could not be oversewn; or lacked folds so they could not be sewn through the fold.

In recent years, however, confidence in the high-quality, internally plasticized polyvinyl acetate adhesives that are used in the double-fanning process has grown based upon experience, and binders have devised improved procedures for spine preparation and adhesive application. Machinery has been developed to automate spine preparation, double-fan gluing, notch filling, and spine lining, improving efficiency and enabling consistent quality.

Working together, libraries and binders have discovered that a great many books and periodicals of varying sizes, weights, and paper types (including coated papers) can be successfully double-fan adhesive bound. Some libraries now request that a high percentage of all volumes be adhesive bound because of the advantages listed in the section "Advantages of Double-fan Adhesive Binding" in this *Guide.*

Regarding the 2" thickness limitation for double-fan adhesive binding, situations may arise where a volume thicker than 2" has extremely narrow margins and must be adhesive bound to preserve openability. In this case, the library can over-ride the suggested thickness limitation. While the binder cannot guarantee the durability of very thick adhesive-bound volumes, they are likely to be sturdy if double-fanning is properly done. Should such a volume fail over time, rebinding using oversewing remains an option, recognizing that information that is printed in the binding margin may be lost.

7.3.1 Preparation

The most important factor in preparing the spine of a volume for double-fan adhesive binding is to ensure that every leaf of the text block is separate from the next. If the text block is not made up of loose leaves, its spine must be milled. Milling is discussed in Section 7.4.1 of this *Guide.*

The process of notching has been used by the library binding industry in Europe since the 1970s and by library binders in the United States since the mid-1980s. See figure 31. Notching increases the surface area of the spine, resulting in greater contact between paper and adhesive. This contact strengthens the bonds formed between leaves and increases the likelihood that all leaves will be securely attached. The notching process is typically incorporated into either a milling/notching machine or an adhesive binding machine. Although notching is very evident before glue and a lining are applied to a spine, once the volume has been glued up and dried, the notching in a well-bound book will be no more obtrusive than sewing holes in a sewn volume.

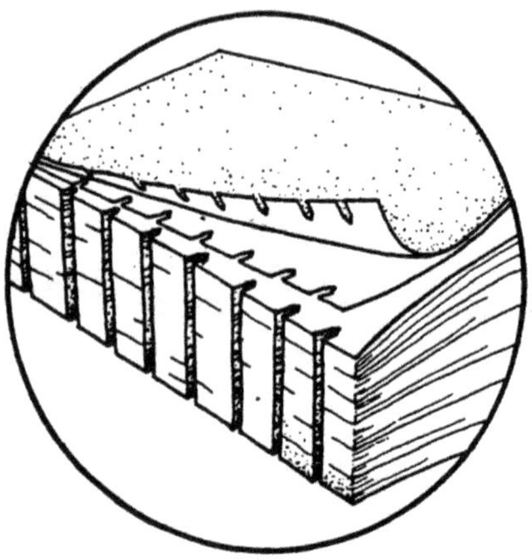

Figure 31. A notched spine.*

Research reported in 1988 by the Dudley Weiss Book Testing Laboratory, Rochester Institute of Technology, suggests that notching can significantly increase the flexing and page-pull strength of double-fan adhesive-bound volumes. This conclusion is supported by test results from the research project, *Performance Measures for Library Binding,* conducted and reported by Barclay Ogden and Robert Strauss; commissioned and published by LBI in 1995.

7.3.2 Attaching Endpapers

No commentary for Section 7.3.2.

7.3.2.1 Endpaper Construction

See figure 32.

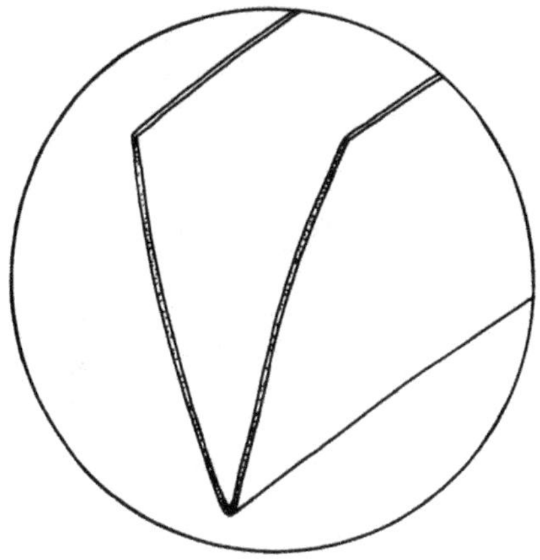

Figure 32. Endpaper for adhesive-bound text blocks.

7.3.3 Fanning and Gluing

The double-fanning process, as described in this section of the *Standard,* is a major factor distinguishing the adhesive binding done by library binders from that done by publishers' binders. During double fanning, the fore edge of the text block is clamped and the binding edge is free to fan, leaf by leaf, against a glue roller. See figure 33. Adhesive is applied to the binding margin of each leaf in a band approximately 1⁄32" wide. Next, the text block is fanned in the opposite direction against the glue roller, and adhesive is applied to the opposite side of the binding margin of each leaf. In this way, each leaf is tipped to the next.

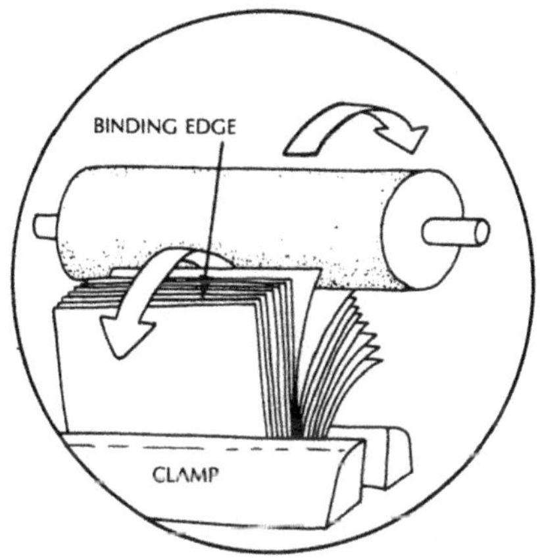

Figure 33. The double-fanning process.

In publishers' binding, the text block is clamped along the binding edge, and the spine is passed over a glue roller. See figure 34. Adhesive is applied to the surface of the spine only, and does not penetrate between leaves to tip them together. As a result, the adhesive bond is far less strong than in double-fan adhesive binding (all other factors being equal).

As has been discussed, publishers' binders typically use hot melt or polyurethane adhesives for adhesive binding. Hot melt and polyurethane adhesives, however, are less reliable. They don't work on all papers all of the time. Library binders use costly cold emulsion adhesives that are very slow drying but retain their flexibility indefinitely.

Selection of a suitable adhesive for double-fan adhesive binding is a major factor in the effectiveness of the technique. The library's best indicator that adhesive is properly chosen and applied is the sturdiness and durability of adhesive bound books. Problems with adhesive bindings will show up with use. If pages detach or text blocks split, adhesives and procedures for double fanning should be discussed with the binder.

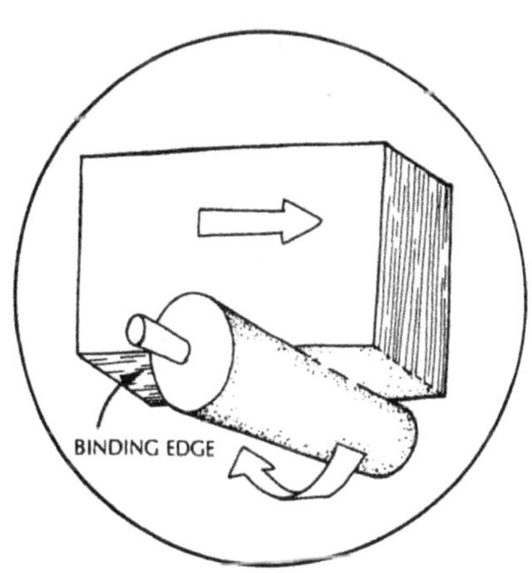

Figure 34. Publishers' adhesive-binding, also known as perfect binding.

7.3.4 Lining

Library binders use modern materials that are very well suited for lining the spines of books. They have both strength and the ability to stretch during rounding and backing. The function of the stretchable spine lining on adhesive-bound volumes is to keep the leaves of the text block tightly consolidated while the glue is wet and to facilitate rounding and backing after the text block dries. The lining material specified in Section 17.2 of the *Standard* was developed to meet both strength and stretchability requirements. In cases where volumes that are sewn through the fold are over 1½" thick, or when those that are adhesive-bound are over 2½" thick, the *Standard* requires that a second spine lining be applied to impart greater dimensional stability. No formal testing has been conducted, however, to justify this requirement, and the improved spine lining material that has been in widespread use during the past decade seems to obviate the need for a second lining.

Advantages of Double-fan Adhesive Binding

- The leaves of a double-fan adhesive-bound volume open to their innermost edges, allowing for easy reading and photocopying.
- Aside from milling, the process uses less than 1⁄16" of binding margin.
- If the volume must be rebound for any reason, it can be done with relatively little loss of additional binding margin.

Disadvantages of Double-fan Adhesive Binding

- Unless the volume is made up of loose leaves, its spine must be milled to free the leaves for fanning. This process removes some of the binding margin.
- If the double-fanning process is not done properly, leaves may be left unattached.
- The durability of a double-fan adhesive binding correlates inversely to the stiffness of the leaves. Text blocks made up of stiff leaves are not ideal candidates for this binding method.
- Sometimes an excessive amount of adhesive will seep between two leaves. This problem is most likely to occur when stiff leaves are interspersed throughout the text block (as when very stiff paper covers are not removed from the issues of a serial volume).
- Careful attention by bindery staff to the application of adhesive can minimize problems.

7.4 Oversewing

There are two questions to consider when determining whether a text block should be oversewn:

- Does the text block exceed 2" in thickness?

  The answer should be yes.

- Is the binding margin at least 5⁄8" wide?

  The answer should be yes.

The description of oversewing that appears in the *Standard* can be understood best by watching an oversewing machine in operation. Ask bindery staff to run the machine through a cycle by hand, and observe the action of the sewing needles and thread.

It is important to note that because oversewing restricts openability, the fact that a volume has adequate binding margins is not necessarily a good reason to oversew it. Instead, oversewing should be used when books are heavy, paper is highly coated, or covers are very stiff.

Where the *Standard* says, "If no other method is appropriate, volumes that have narrow margins may be oversewn on a machine that has been modified by adding a narrow sewing plate," it refers to a technique that pre-dated the less invasive double-fan adhesive binding.

Although, as the *Standard* suggests, oversewing can be done by hand, hand oversewing is reserved for volumes that are too tall to sew by machine. Most oversewing machines are unable to sew volumes more than 15" tall.

Where the *Standard* reads, "Medium and large size text blocks that are oversewn by hand shall be sewn onto tapes," there is no reason to hand oversew medium-sized volumes. The tapes referred to are the same type as those used for sewing through the fold. See Section 7.2.2.1 of the *Standard* and this *Guide*.

7.4.1 Preparation

Although the *Standard* states that "no more than ⅛" of the binding margin shall be removed [by milling]," the objective being to remove as little of the binding margin as possible, if a volume is composed of very thick signatures, it must be milled more than once in order to cut the folds of all leaves. See figure 35. Occasionally, publishers' adhesive bindings must also be milled more than once because adhesive bleeds deeply between leaves.

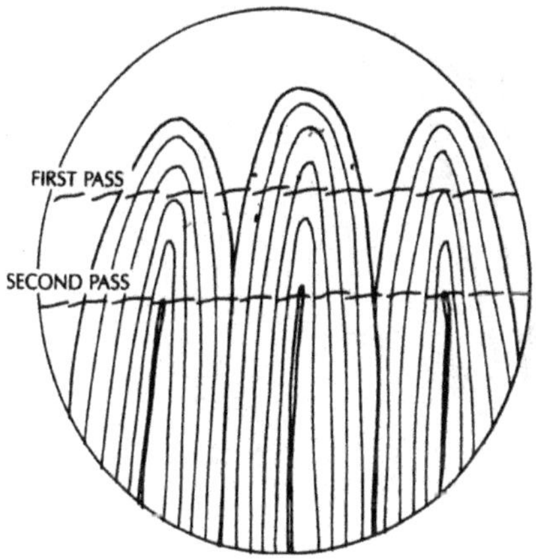

Figure 35. Thick signatures require double milling.

Because milling volumes with thick signatures often sacrifices more than ⅛" of the binding margin, it should be avoided if possible. Serial volumes made up of thick signatures can be sewn through the fold, and monographs that have thick signatures can sometimes be recased.

7.4.2 Attaching Endpapers

After the text block has been milled to separate the leaves (if necessary), the oversewing machine operator feeds the leaves into the sewing machine in thin sections (thin piles), one after another, each time depressing a foot pedal that activates the sewing needles. First, an endpaper and the first section of leaves are sewn through twice. The second section is placed on top of the first and is also sewn through twice. Each successive section is placed on top of the growing text block and is sewn through once. The last section, along with the second endpaper, is sewn through three times to lock the sewing.

Because oversewing machinery automatically positions sections at a 45° angle to the vertical sewing needles, with every sewing stitch, sewing thread passes through the topmost section and the two or three below it, but not through the entire stack. See figure 36.

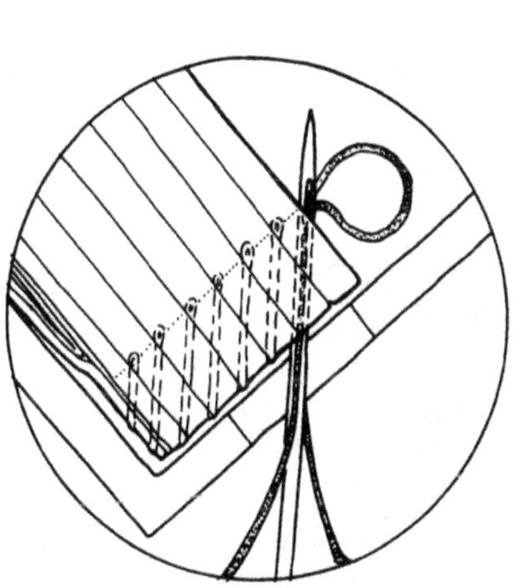
Figure 36. Passage of thread through an oversewn volume.

Although the *Standard* states that "all volumes shall be divided into uniform sections approximately 1⁄16" thick," in practice, splitting into sections up to ⅛" thick appears to be perfectly acceptable. Sections of ⅛" may, in fact be preferable, since the thicker the section, the fewer the number of times it is sewn through—and therefore the less heavily it is perforated. When paper is coated, thin sections are particularly problematic.

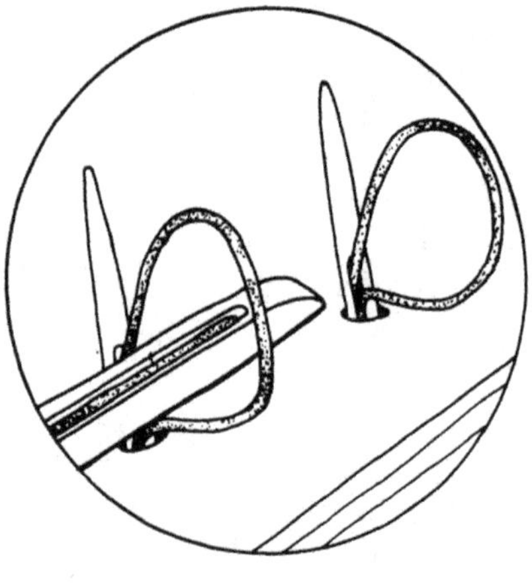

Figure 37. Shuttle threads passing through loops.

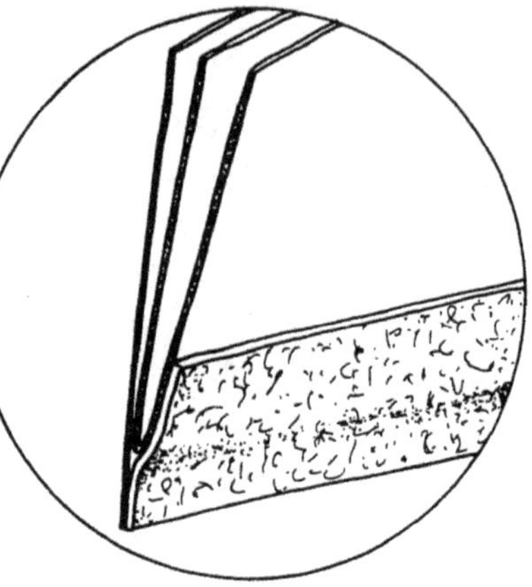

Figure 38. Oversewn endpaper.

The *Standard* describes two methods for tipping one section to the next along the binding margin. Tipping hides the shuttle threads that otherwise would be visible in the finished volume at every juncture where one section ends and another begins. See figure 37. Tipping is done for aesthetic purposes and to secure the shuttle thread. The description of the coating of shuttle thread with methyl cellulose may suggest that the process is performed by hand. This is not the case. Oversewing machines are usually fitted with two small paste pots through which shuttle threads pass on their way to two shuttle needles. The very rarely used alternative process, application of "a thin line of paste along the binding margin [of] the top sheet of each section prior to sewing," can be done with a mechanical device called a tipping machine.

7.4.2.1 Endpaper Construction

The first endpaper listed in this section, often referred to as the "oversew" endpaper, was used almost exclusively by the library binding industry until about 1980. See figure 38. This endpaper is folded back on itself so that it will hinge at the binding edge. See figure 39. The endpaper traditionally used for side-sewn volumes has now gained acceptance as a viable alternative for oversewn volumes as well. See figure 40. When the "side sew" endpaper is used for oversewn volumes, boards must be cut approximately ¼" narrower than the text block as specified in Section 12.3.2 of the *Standard.* The resulting "wide-hinge case" has joints ¼" wider than those of a traditional case. See figure 41 and Section 12.3.1 of the *Standard.* Also see the glossary of the *Standard* for a definition of "joint."

Use of the side-sew endpaper for oversewn volumes is favored by some librarians because it eliminates the hard edge created when the oversew endpaper is folded back, as shown in figure 39c. As acidic

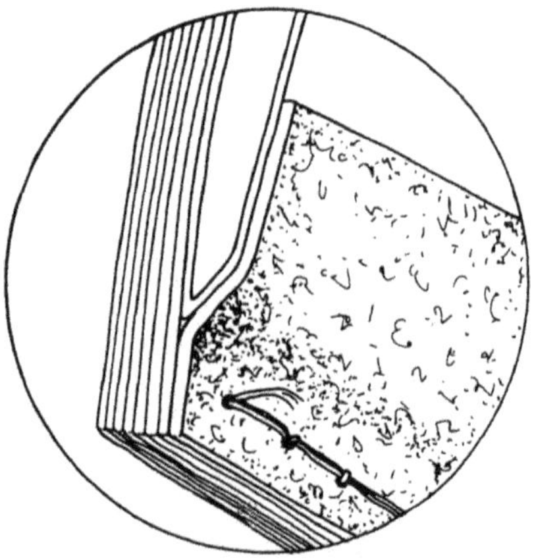

Figure 39a. Oversewn endpaper sewn onto text block.

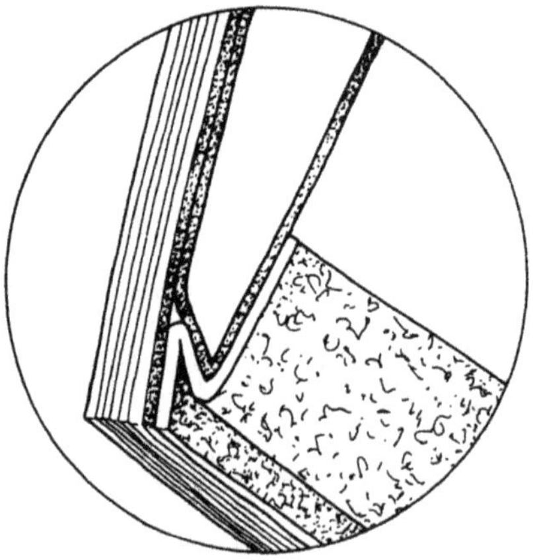

Figure 39b. Oversewn endpaper sewn on and folded back

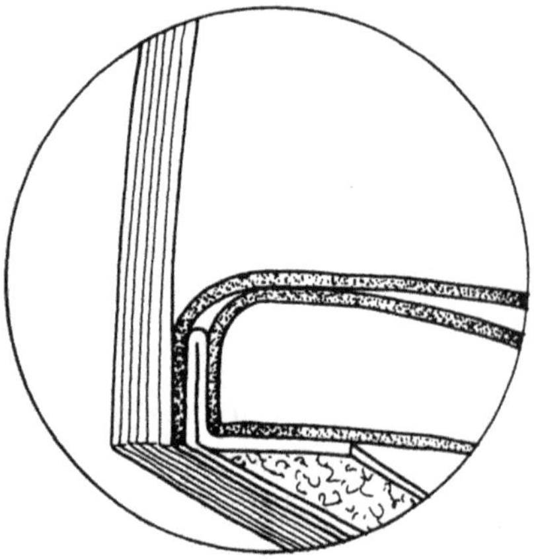

Figure 39c. Oversewn endpaper sewn on, folded back and tipped down.

paper ages, it sometimes breaks as it flexes against this edge. It deserves mention that from a production standpoint, it would be very difficult for a binder to switch to a wide joint for oversewn volumes only. The major technical changes necessitated by conversion (cutting boards smaller, making the space between the inlay and boards wider, and fitting the building-in machine with thicker jaws) are not easily applied on an item-by-item basis and may result in surcharges.

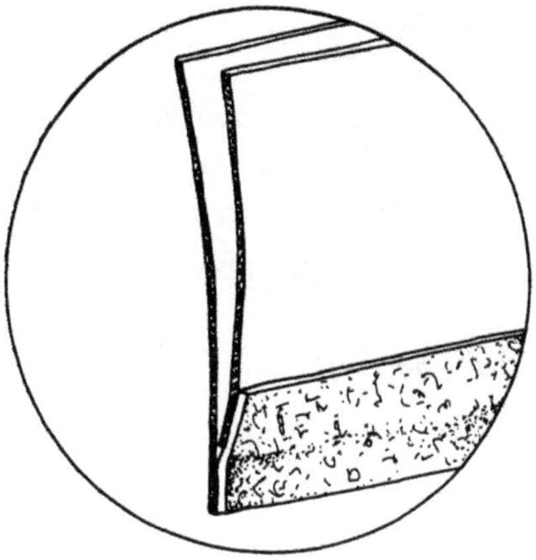

Figure 40. Side-sewn endpaper.

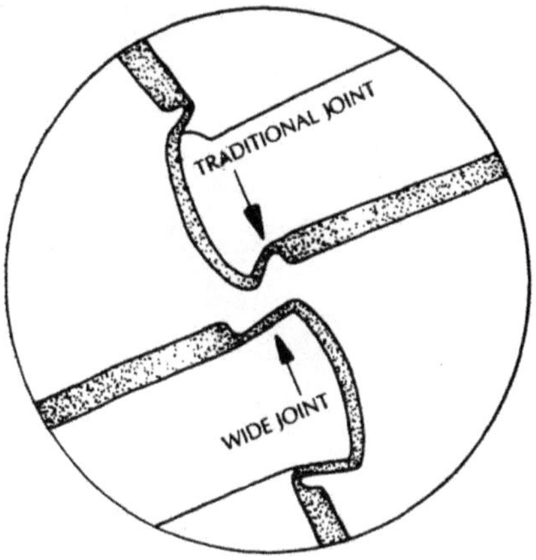

Figure 41. Traditional joint and wide joint.

Advantage of Oversewing

- When the paper in an oversewn volume is in good condition, the leaf attachment is very secure.

Disadvantages of Oversewing

- Unless it can be separated into sections without milling (as in the case of a loose-leaf volume), the spine of a book must be milled before it can be fed into an oversewing machine in sections. This milling removes some of the binding margin.
- Oversewing is essentially a form of side sewing. Thread passes obliquely through the binding margin of the text block, inhibiting the leaves from opening all the way to their innermost edges. See figure 42. Oversewn volumes sometimes have poor openability characteristics, particularly in cases where pages are printed with the grain of the paper running perpendicular rather than parallel to the spine (i.e., when the paper is printed "cross-grain"). To observe the functionality of the oversewn volume firsthand, place several such monographs on a work surface, open each, and let go of it. Many (particularly smaller volumes) will snap shut. Another disadvantage of oversewing is that print near the binding margin is often difficult to read and cannot be photocopied completely. See figure 43.
- Oversewing intrudes into the binding margin a full 3⁄16". Considering that approximately 1⁄8" has already been removed during spine milling, the overall loss of binding margin is significant—approximately 5⁄16". When a volume is oversewn a second time (usually to incorporate a missing issue) in most cases an additional 1⁄8" to 1⁄4" of binding margin is lost when the original oversewing thread is cut away (usually by a guillotine), and an additional 3⁄16" is lost when the text block is restitched. The total margin lost can be as much as 3⁄4".

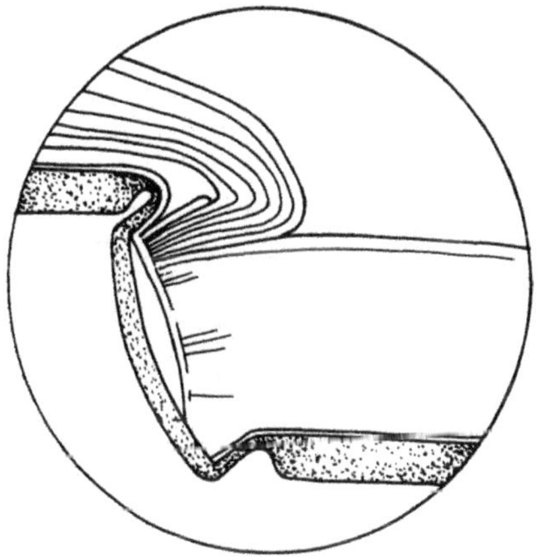

Figure 42. Restricted openability of an oversewn volume.

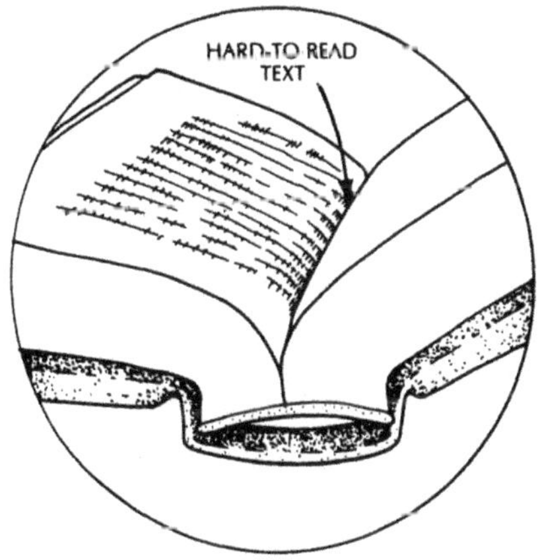

Figure 43. Hard-to-read text near the binding margin in many oversewn volumes.

- As a result of the oversewing process, the binding margin of each leaf of the text block is pierced in many places. See figure 44. These perforations weaken the text paper. The outcome may not be noticeable in new volumes but in older volumes where the paper has become brittle, leaves sometimes break along the line of sewing.
- Oversewing is more expensive.

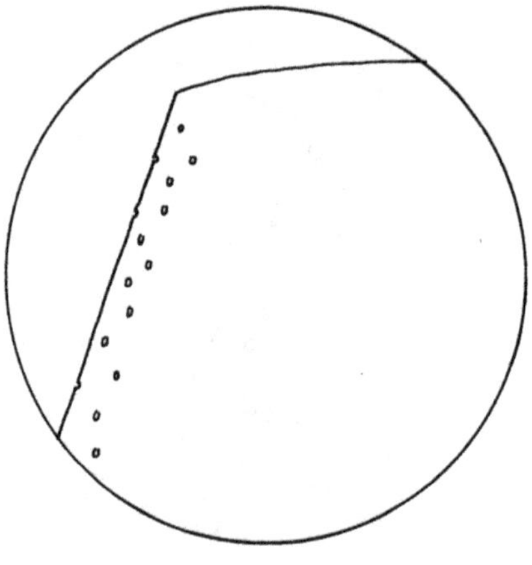

Figure 44. The perforated edge of a leaf that has been oversewn.

7.4.3 Sewing

No commentary for Section 7.4.3.

7.5 Side Sewing

For a discussion of the machine that is used for side sewing and an illustration of the lock stitch, see the last paragraph of Section 7.2.2.2 of this *Guide* and figure 26. While some industrial side-sewing machines can sew through a volume several inches thick, first drilling holes through the binding margin and then stitching, the *Standard* places an upper limit of ½" on the thickness of a side-sewn volume. In side sewing, the thread passes perpendicularly through the binding margin of the text block (see figure 45) inhibiting the leaves from opening all the way to their innermost edges (see figure 46). Side sewing should not be perceived as the method of choice for thin volumes simply because it is recommended only for thin volumes. In fact, single-signature pamphlets, music scores for example, should be sewn through the fold. All other thin volumes can be recased or double-fan adhesive bound.

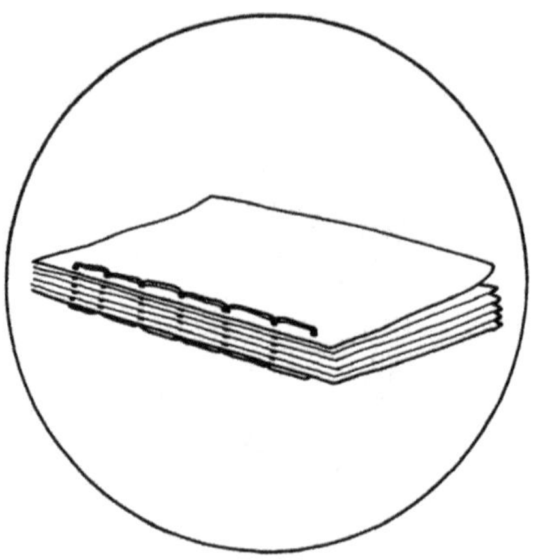

Figure 45. Thread passing perpendicularly through the binding margin of a side-sewn text block.

7.5.1 Preparation

All staples must be removed before side sewing because as mentioned earlier, they rust when it becomes humid and can erode the paper surrounding them.

The folds of signatures need not be trimmed away from a volume before side sewing, because the entire text block is sewn in a single pass.

7.5.2 Attaching the Endpapers

No commentary for Section 7.5.2.

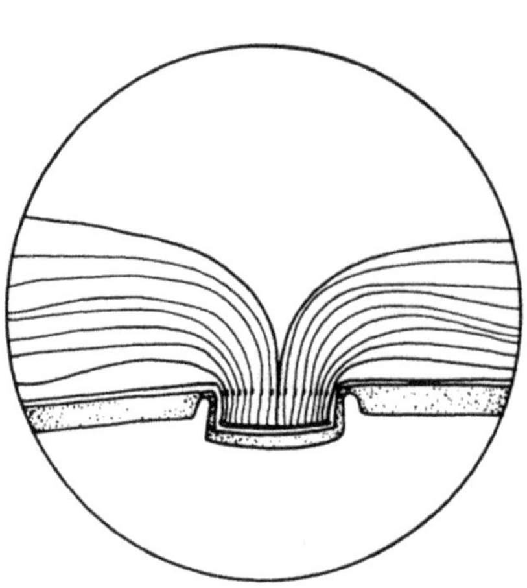

Figure 46. Restricted openability of a side-sewn text block.

7.5.2.1 Endpaper Construction

Endpapers used for side sewing are the same as those used for oversewing. See Section 7.4.2.1 of the *Standard* and this *Guide.*

Advantage of Side Sewing

- The leaves of side-sewn volumes are very securely attached. For this reason, children's books are often side sewn.

Disadvantages of Side Sewing

- Side sewing restricts openability.
- A ¾" binding margin is necessary.

8. Trimming the Text Block

Trimming the fore edge, head, and tail of a text block is standard procedure for most library binderies, except in cases where doing so would remove text. Some libraries, however, in keeping with overall preservation policy request that all monographs be left untrimmed or that all volumes including serials be left untrimmed.

The *Standard* states that "trimmed edges shall be smooth and without knife marks." These marks are created by nicks in the guillotine blade that are made when staples, paper clips, and metallic security strips are cut. Libraries can assist binders by adhering security strips and badges no closer than ½" from the head, tail, and fore edge of a text block and by removing paper clips and other metallic objects from volumes. While the binder should change blades frequently, it is inevitable that minor knife marks will sometimes occur.

Advantages of a No-trim Policy

- Margins protect text from dirt and wear, and trimming them reduces this protection. A no-trim policy leaves margins intact.
- When margins are left untrimmed, the original size of the leaves and print-to-margin ratio is unchanged, thus preserving aesthetic characteristics and bibliographic integrity.
- Many modern publications are printed with extremely narrow margins. In some cases, there is no margin at all (e.g., when illustrations and charts bleed to the edges of pages, as they do in *National Geographic*). In addition, margin and issue sizes can vary in serials, making it difficult to check them for potential trimming problems; and folded plates are easily missed during collation. A no-trim policy ensures that narrow margins will not be further reduced and that text, illustrations, and the folds of folded plates and other inserts will not be cut away.

Disadvantages of a No-trim Policy

- When monographs are left untrimmed, text blocks look the same when they come back from the bindery as they did when they were sent out. If the edges are soiled or tattered, they remain that way. A solution to this problem is to specify trimming only when needed. Trimming then becomes the exception rather than the rule.
- When serials are left untrimmed and issue sizes vary, edges can be quite choppy.

Some binders levy an extra charge per volume for a no-trim policy for the following reasons:

Occasionally the text blocks of monographs and serial issues are not squarely cut, and do not fit well into square cases. Trimming makes a text block perfectly square and facilitates case making and casing in. An untrimmed text block is more difficult for the binder to process.

When selecting endpapers, binders choose the size nearest to, and just larger than, the text block. In cases where text blocks are trimmed on a guillotine, the new endpapers are cut simultaneously. When text blocks are left untrimmed, however, endpapers must be hand trimmed in a separate process. (This should be done using a special cutting machine; scissors do not always make neat, straight cuts.) The extra step is time consuming.

Because untrimmed text blocks are often untidy, librarians and library users can mistakenly attribute them to unfinished or sloppy binding. When a library makes the decision to switch to a no-trim policy (particularly for serials), the rationale for doing so must be communicated clearly to library staff and occasionally, patrons.

9. Gluing the Spine

The *Standard* states, "Polyvinyl acetate adhesives shall be applied to the spines of all sewn text blocks prior to rounding and backing." In fact, the spines of volumes that have been sewn through the fold or recased must be glued *before* trimming so that signatures will not shift after trimming or be uneven at the head, tail, or fore edge.

10. Spine Treatment

Rounding and backing has traditionally been considered an integral part of library binding procedures, but flat-back library binding entered the mainstream in the 1970s and competed for primacy. See figure 47.

Two comparative studies of the technique conducted at the Dudley A. Weiss Book Testing Laboratory (Rochester Institute of Technology) in the 1980s were inconclusive. Research conducted in 1995, however, concluded that rounding and backing does enhance the durability of a binding, especially when it is large or heavy. See Section 7.3.1.

At present, some binders continue to round and back all volumes, convinced of the validity of these findings and believing that the process enhances the appearance, strength, and openability of volumes. Others make a case that rounding and backing can damage sewing thread, weak or heavily coated paper, the adhesive bond in double-fan adhesive binding, and threads in volumes that are sewn through the fold. In fact, each approach appears to be a viable option under some circumstances.

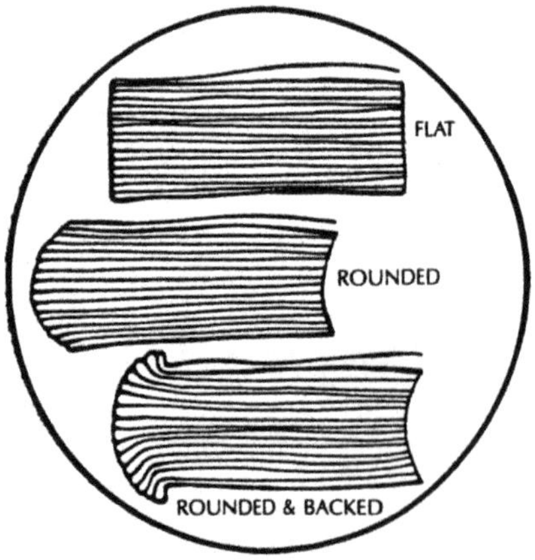

Figure 47. Flat-backed, rounded, and rounded-and-backed text blocks.*

Rounding and backing is most often done on a hydraulically operated machine that must be adjusted to accommodate volumes of different thicknesses. When a volume does not round and back well the first time, some binderies reback using hand-operated equipment.

Some volumes can *only* be processed using hand-operated equipment, including those with fragile paper, weak sewing thread, or already-rounded spines. Eliminating this step across the board reduces costs, while determining which volumes to round and back on an item-by-item basis can increase costs.

Some volumes are best left flat backed, as described in Section 10.2 of the *Standard*. Other volumes are improved by rounding and backing. For example, the rounding and backing can enhance openability when paper is stiff and inflexible, because it scores each leaf near the binding edge, parallel with the spine of the volume. Rounding and backing may also help to prevent large volumes from becoming misshapen.

Whether the rounding and backing improves openability and durability—whether it damages a volume or enhances it—varies from volume to volume depending on a complex mix of physical characteristics and the precise way in which the process is executed.

The *Standard* specifies rounding and backing for all but the following types of text blocks:

- Volumes with multiple-signatures thicker than ¼" (as is sometimes the case with serial issues). For all practical purposes backing these is impossible.
- Rounded and backed volumes that are being recased. These are best "re-rounded and backed only if they are poorly shaped and have strong sewing thread and paper." Since there is no reliable way to measure the strength of the thread used by publishers' binders, volumes that are already rounded and backed are usually best left as is.
- Because of their light weight, most text blocks that are less than ½" thick do not require rounding and backing.
- In no case should volumes with fragile paper be rounded and backed, as text paper can fracture and tear as a result.

10.1 Rounding and Backing

No commentary for Section 10.1

10.1.1 Process

Rounding and backing should be symmetrical. The shoulders must be smaller than the board thickness so that they do not protrude beyond the text block. See figure 48. Modern rounder-and-backers produce excellent results but expectations must be reasonable. Every book is different from the next and results will vary.

To some extent, problems can be controlled by keeping machinery in optimal condition and by using hand-operated roller backers and a hammer to improve results.

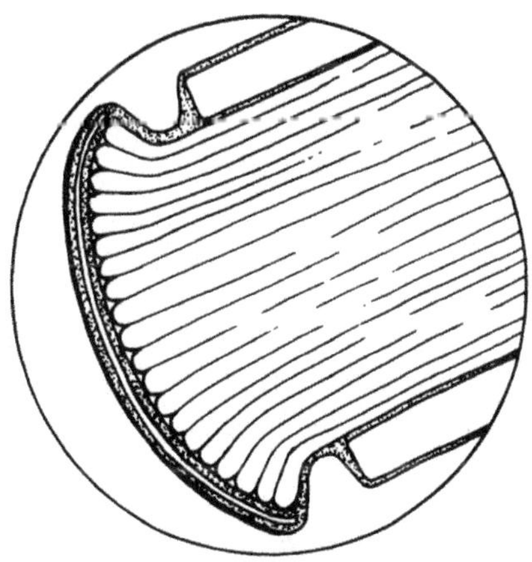

Figure 48. Properly backed text block. Shoulders equal the thickness of the text block plus the board.

10.2 Flat-Backed Text Blocks

No commentary for Section 10.2

11. Lining the Spine

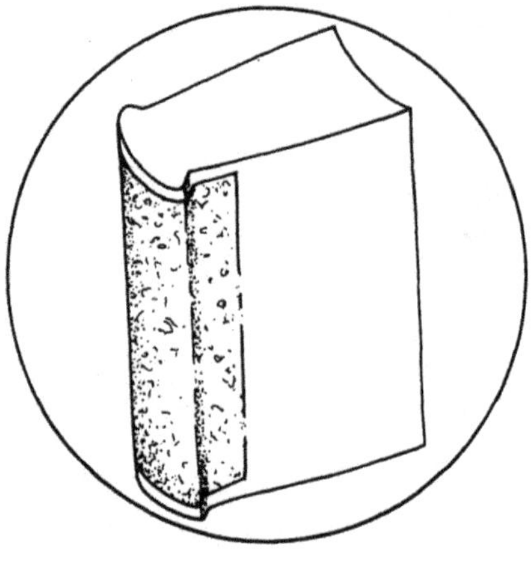

Figure 49. Spine lined with spine-lining cloth.

The *Standard* states, "The spines of all text blocks shall be lined with spine lining material." See figure 49. For double-fan adhesive-bound volumes, lining happens as part of the process of attaching the leaves. See Section 7.3.4 of the *Standard.*

The quality of the material that is used for spine lining and the evenness and tightness of its adhesion are critical to the strength and durability of a library-bound volume. The spine lining reinforces the sewing or adhesive structure, and it strengthens the joints of the case so that they can withstand repeated flexing. (It is in the joint area that publishers' bindings typically fail). The spine lining material used by library binders is much sturdier than the lining used by publishers' binders. As a result, the text blocks of library-bound volumes rarely pull away from their cases.

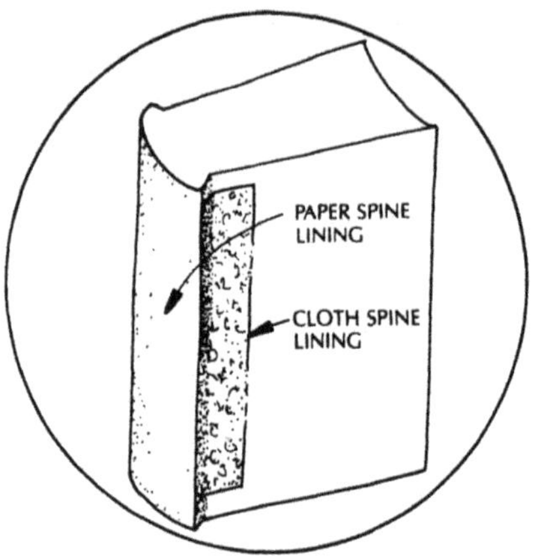

Figure 50. Spine linings for large and heavy text blocks.

Another function of the lining is to stiffen the spine a bit, reducing its tendency to be wobbly, become misshapen, or cave in. Because very large and heavy text blocks that are sewn through the fold or recased are more likely to develop problems, they require an additional layer of spine lining—preferably 60-pound (or heavier) alkaline cover stock. See figure 50.

The *Standard* also describes a method for lining the spines of thick volumes with a double layer of spine lining material. See figure 51. This method is less effective than lining with 60-pound paper because the paper has greater dimensional stability.

12. Making the Case

No commentary for Section 12.

12.1 Cutting the Covering Material

No commentary for Section 12.1

12.2 Lettering the Covering Material

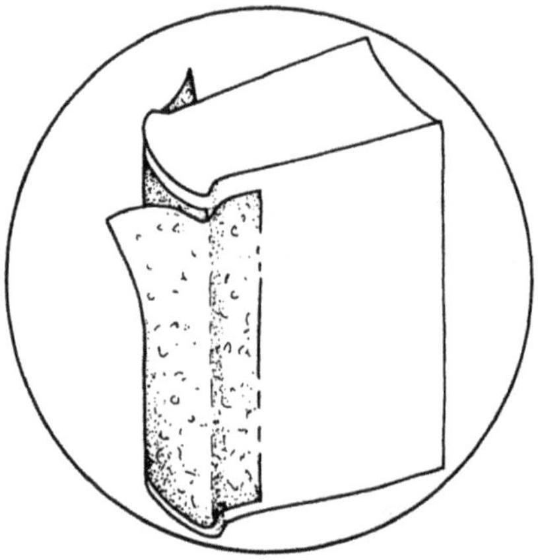

Figure 51. Double-cloth spine lining for large and heavy text blocks.

The *Standard* states that lettering shall be stamped with "adequate pressure, temperature, and dwell." This refers to the functionality of stamping machinery. It means that type must be pressed into covering material using adequate pressure, must be heated to the proper temperature, and must remain in contact with the covering material for an adequate period of time to ensure proper adhesion. Specifications cannot be stated precisely because of the variety of equipment in use, and the fact that pressure, temperature, and dwell can be varied in relation to one another to achieve similar results.

Binders use the spine stamping information supplied by the library. The library can improve the binder's efficiency and cut costs by specifying the shortest title that will serve to distinguish a volume or set of volumes from others on the shelf. This truncation is especially important for government publications, complex series, and other volumes with long titles.

For periodicals, the library can expect the first line of each panel (title, variable information, and call number) to line up, but the layout of words may vary from volume to volume if the thickness of the volumes varies. On the thinnest volumes, it may be necessary to letter vertically. For thin volumes with long titles, it may be necessary to move the title or call number to the front cover or to shorten the title. It is important for the library and the binder to develop a policy for handling situations where lettering will not fit on the spine of a volume and to include this policy in the customer profile. See appendix F.

12.3 Selecting and Cutting Boards

Although the practice of binding flush with the bottom of the case is discussed briefly in Section 12.3 of the *Standard,* it is best understood by referring to Section 13 of both the *Standard* and this *Guide.*

The *Standard* does not set forth specific guidelines for selecting binder's board of appropriate thickness for the size and weight of the text block being bound. Although the *Standard* states that at least two (preferably three) thicknesses of board should be stocked, given new performance-based specifications for board, a choice of one or two thicknesses is adequate to accommodate library-bound volumes.

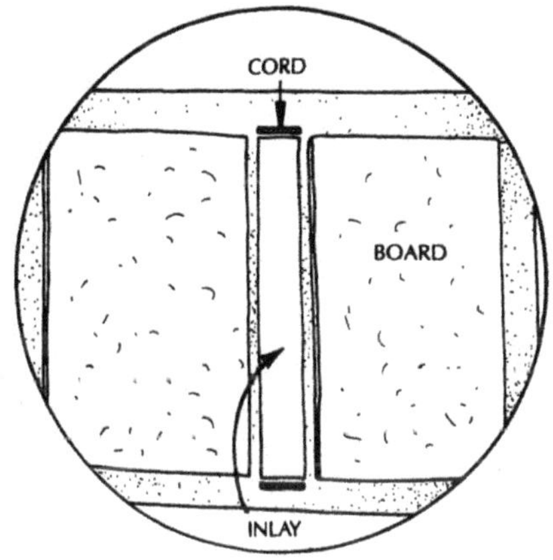

Figure 52. Cord placed at the head and tail of the inlay.

12.3.1 Narrow-Hinge Cases

No commentary for Section 12.3.1

12.3.2 Wide-Hinge Cases

No commentary for Section 12.3.2

12.4 Selecting and Cutting the Inlay

The inlay and the adhesive that attaches it to the inside of the covering material stiffen the spine of the case and ensure that it remains smooth. By preventing wrinkles and creases, they also help to keep lettering from wearing off.

12.5 Assembling the Case

Prior to publication of the 2000 edition, the *Standard* required that a piece of cord be placed at the head and tail of the inlay before the covering material is turned over it and glued down. See figure 52. This cord gives a finished appearance to the case. Another approach, common in publishers' hard cover bindings, is to apply headbands. Rather than being built into the case, they are adhered to the head and tail of the spine of the text block See figure 53. While cords give a volume a more finished appearance, the relative strength of this and other reinforcing methods has been shown not to improve the strength of the endcap. For this reason, the *Standard* states that the inlay may be left

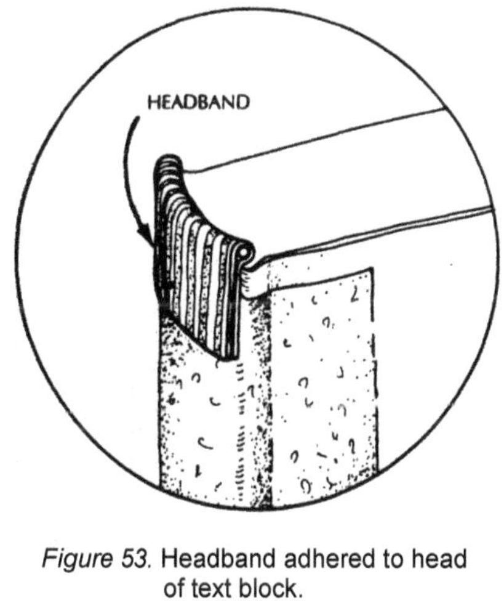

Figure 53. Headband adhered to head of text block.

plain—without additional reinforcement. The covering materials used in library bindings have remarkably high tear strength. See Sections 18.1 and 18.1.1 of the *Standard.*

The *Standard* specifies two methods for turning covering material over the corners of the case. For the library corner, each corner of the covering material is folded down onto the boards at a 45° angle and the material along the head, tail, and fore edges of the case is then turned in. See figure 54.

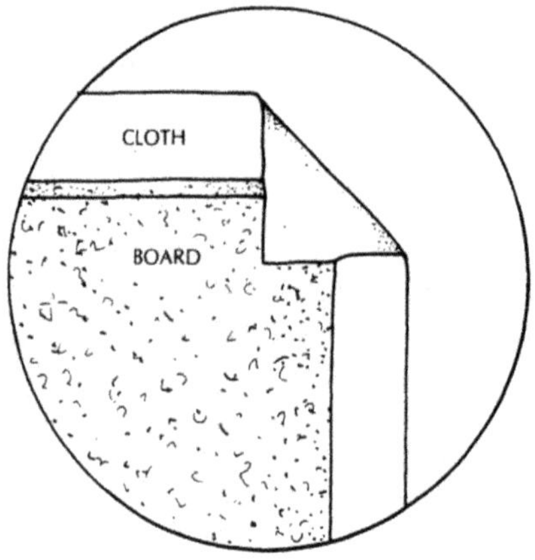

Figure 54a. Library corner, step 1.

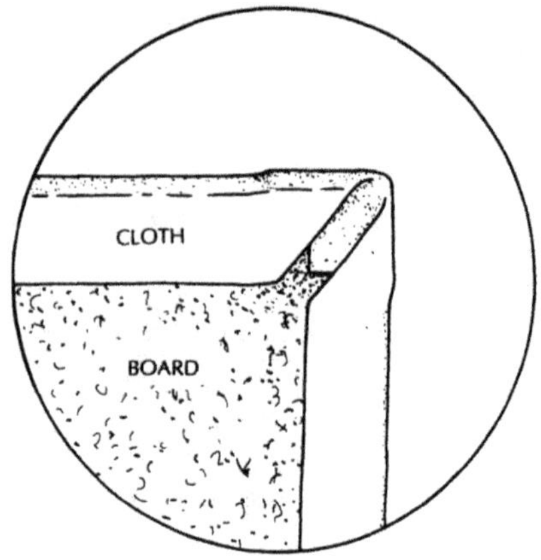

Figure 54b. Library corner, step 2.

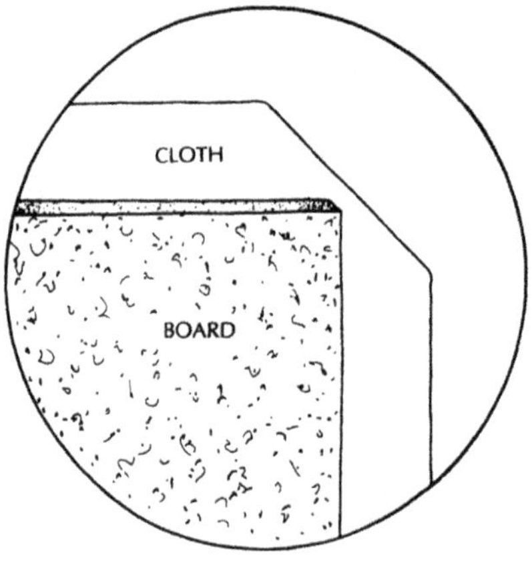

Figure 55a. Traditional corner, step 1.

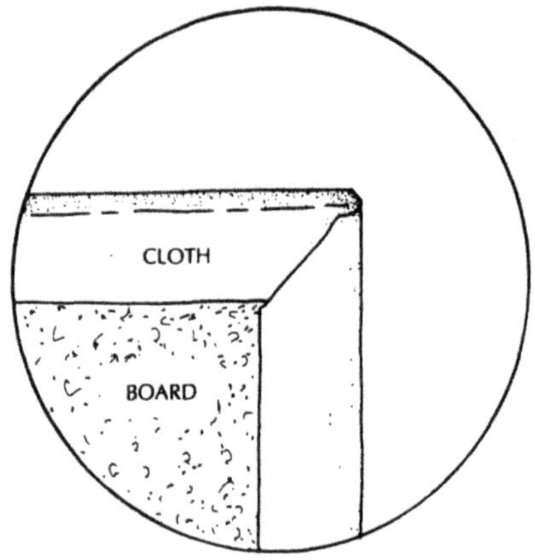

Figure 55b. Traditional corner, step 2.

The traditional corner, which is typically used by publishers' binders, involves cutting away the tips of the corners of the covering material at a 45° angle and then turning in the material along the head, tail, and fore edge. See figure 55. Both types of corners were tested for durability in the LBI study *Performance Measures for Library Binding.* Testing found that they wear equally well.

12.6 Corners

No commentary for Section 12.6

12.6.1 Library Corners

No commentary for Section 12.6.1.

12.6.2 Traditional Corners

No commentary for Section 12.6.2.

13. Casing In

The adhesive bond between the text block and the case is critical in the library binding process. The *Standard* acknowledges that heavy or thick text blocks tend to sag in their cases, which weakens bindings in the joint area. See figure 56. Ideally, such text blocks would be split into two volumes so that each is no thicker than 2", but for bibliographic reasons this is not always possible. By eliminating the square at the tail of the case, the text block rests solidly on the shelf and is less likely to become loose in the joint area or to cave in at the spine over time. See figure 57. While the tails of flush-bound text blocks may become soiled when book shelves are dirty, experience has shown that heavy text blocks bound with a ⅛" square inevitably sag to the shelf in any case and become soiled.

The library may specify flush binding as part of special instructions for treating a particular volume or may specify flush binding for an entire category of materials (e.g., for all text blocks over 1½" thick). Because binding flush with the bottom of the case requires special handling in the bindery (e.g., boards must be cut ⅛" taller than the text block rather than ¼" taller) libraries should expect binders to charge extra for this treatment.

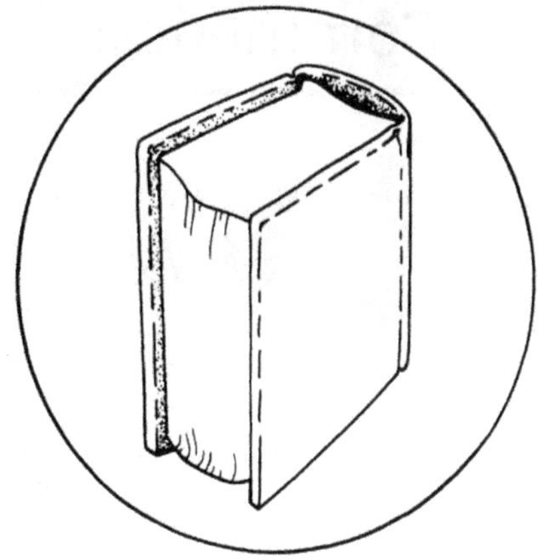

Figure 56. Fore edge of a sagging text block in a traditional case.

Figure 57. Fore edge of a text block bound flush to the case.

Commentary on the *Standard*

MATERIALS SPECIFICATIONS

Some of the specifications in the materials section of the *Standard* are nonspecific. This lack of specificity reflects both the modest amount of research and testing that has been conducted on materials to date and the proven durability of the materials that are used by library binders.

14. Inspection

No commentary for Section 14.

15. Paper

No commentary for Section 15.

15.1 Endpapers

No commentary for Section 15.1.

15.1.1 Paper Composition

No commentary for Section 15.1.1.

15.1.2 Basis Weight

No commentary for Section 15.1.2.

15.1.3 Mechanical Characteristics

No commentary for Section 15.1.3.

15.2 Papers for Stubbing, Pockets, Additional Spine Lining Reinforcement, and Setting Out Inserts

The *Standard* lists papers used for stubbing, pockets, and setting out inserts as having to meet *ANSI—Permanence of Paper for Printed Library Materials* (*ANSI/NISO Z39.48-1992 [R2002]*) or its most recent edition. All other papers used in the library binding process should also meet that standard or its most current edition.

15.3 Inlays

No commentary for Section 15.3.

16. Cover Board

No commentary for Section 16.

16.1 General Requirements

No commentary for Section 16.1.

16.1.1 Surface

No commentary for Section 16.1.1.

16.1.2 Direction of Grain

No commentary for Section 16.1.2.

16.1.3 Density

No commentary for Section 16.1.3.

16.1.4 Internal Bond

No commentary for Section 16.1.4.

16.1.5 Moisture Content

No commentary for Section 16.1.5.

16.2 Thickness, Bursting Strength, and Flexural Properties

No commentary for Section 16.2.

16.2.1 Thickness Tolerance

No commentary for Section 16.2.1.

17. Reinforcing Material

No commentary for Section 17.

17.1 Reinforcing Material for Endpapers

No commentary for Section 17.1.

17.1.1 Reinforcing Material for Folded Endpapers

No commentary for Section 17.1.1.

17.1.2 Reinforcing Material for Endpapers for Side-Sewn Books

No commentary for Section 17.1.2.

17.2 Material for Lining the Spines of All Text Blocks

The material used for lining the spines of double-fan adhesive-bound text blocks is engineered to be strong enough to reinforce the leaf attachment and to provide durable attachment of the case to the text block—even after rounding and backing.

18. Covering Materials

No commentary for Section 18.

18.1 Covering Materials

No commentary for Section 18.1.

18.1.1 Exceptions

For several decades, aqueous acrylic-coated Group F buckram has been the preferred covering material for library binding. The *Standard* states that Group C-1 Book Cloth and other alternative covering materials may be substituted with approval from the customer.

As of 2006, Groups C and C-1 cloth have been superseded by the single Group C/C-1 product. Although Group C/C-1 and Type II covering materials are less bulky than Group F buckram, they are less strong and less resistant to water, dirt, grease, and abrasion. These alternatives should be used only for binding paperbacks and other small, lightweight volumes.

19. Adhesives

No commentary for Section 19.

19.1 Adhesives for All Purposes

Binders use a variety of adhesives for different purposes. Because there is no other practical way for libraries to monitor their type and quality, the *Standard* discusses adhesive performance, since performance is observable and measurable.

19.2 Adhesive for Double-Fan Adhesive Binding, Gluing the Spine, and Lining the Spine

Cross-linking occurs when atoms or small molecules link long-chain molecules together to create network polymers. The more cross-linking that occurs within the molecular structure of a material, the more hard and rigid that material becomes. Because the adhesives used for double-fan adhesive binding and gluing and lining the spine must remain flexible to be effective, cross-linking is highly undesirable.

Also important is the compatibility of these adhesives with each other and with the adhesive used for case making. While research results aid in determining what combinations are optimal, the degree of soundness of the finished binding is the best indicator of success. For a discussion of the adhesives used for double-fan adhesive binding, see Section 7.3.3 of this *Guide.*

19.3 Adhesive for Making the Case

High-grade animal glue and polyvinyl acetate (PVA) emulsion adhesive may perform equally well for case making, but test data confirm that a PVA case-making adhesive bonds better to the PVA adhesive used to case in the text block, thus producing strong joints. Animal glue, when tested, did not bond to polyvinyl acetate emulsion adhesive as well as two polyvinyl acetate emulsion adhesives bonded to each other.

19.4 Adhesive for Casing In

No commentary for Section 19.4.

19.5 Additional Requirements for Alternate Adhesives

No commentary for Section 19.5.

19.5.1 Strength of Leaf Attachment

No commentary for Section 19.5.1.

19.5.2 Openability

No commentary for Section 19.5.2.

19.5.3 Joint Strength

No commentary for Section 19.5.3.

20. Thread

Binders use a wide variety of threads for oversewing, sewing through the fold, and side sewing, including cotton, cotton-covered polyester, and nylon. The criteria for suitability are that the thread not tangle or break during the sewing process or break when a bound volume receives very heavy use. While no research has been conducted to determine which of the threads used by the library binding industry is best, all threads used by library binders have proven to be adequately strong.

20.1 Thread for Oversewing

No commentary for Section 20.1.

20.2 Thread for Sewing Through the Fold

No commentary for Section 20.2.

20.3 Thread for Side Sewing

No commentary for Section 20.3.

21. Sewing Tapes

No commentary for Section 21.

22. Lettering Foil

No commentary for Section 22.

23. Exceptions

No commentary for Section 23.

Appendix A

*Decision Tree 1: **Is Binding Necessary?***

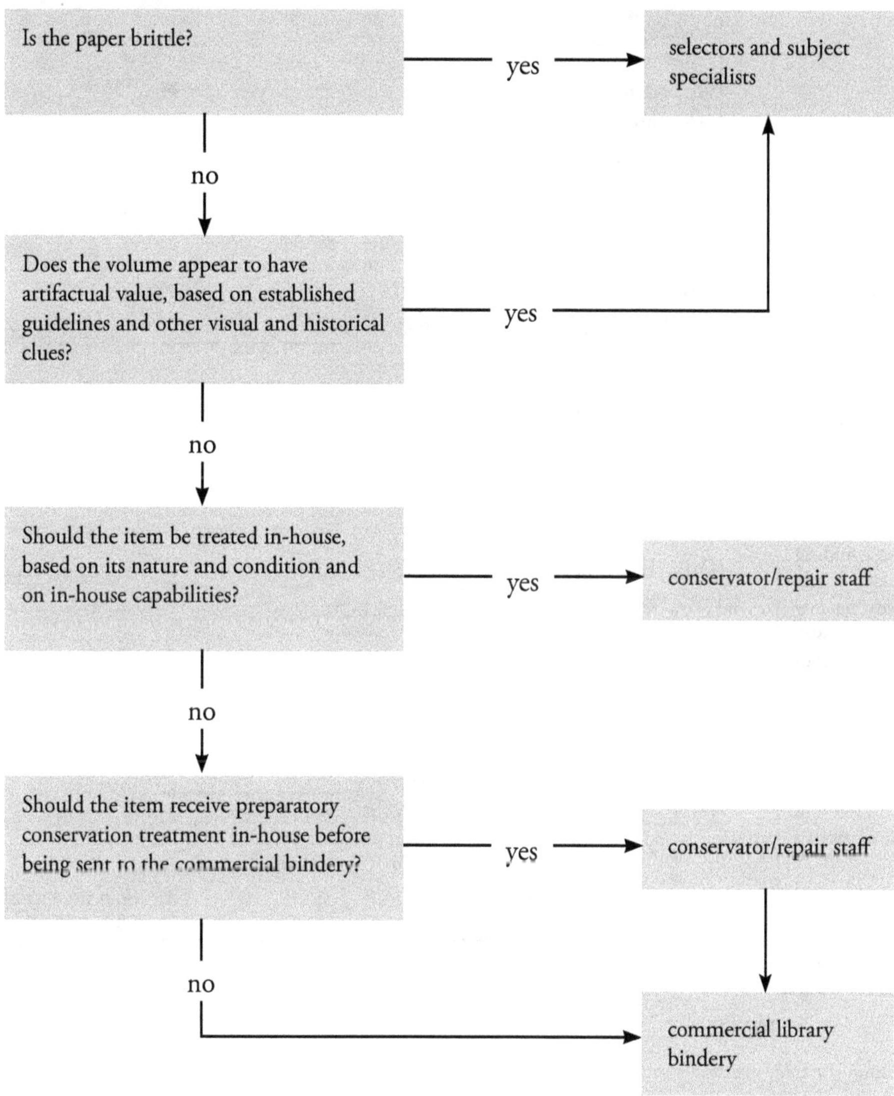

Decision Tree 2: ***Binding Monographs***

Sewing
Is the text block sewn?[a]
Is the original sewing intact?
Is the number of stitches adequate for the size of the volume?

— yes → recase

no ↓

Signatures
Is the text block made up of separate signatures (a group of unattached signatures)?
Are the folds of the signatures intact?[b]

— yes → sew through the fold

no ↓

Thin Text Block
Is the text block 2" thick or less?

— yes → double-fan adhesive bind

no ↓

Thick Text Block
Is the text block more than 2" thick?
Are the margins at least 5/8" wide?

— yes → oversew[c]

no → Split the text block, alter bibliographic records, and double-fan adhesive bind each part; double-fan adhesive bind the text block as is; or box.[d]

Cost-saving Options

- Reserve recasing for volumes that cannot be double-fan adhesive bound because milling the spine would damage fragile paper, remove already-narrow binding margins, or cut away plates that bleed to the inner edges of pages.

  Using these criteria, the majority of volumes that are potential candidates for recasing would be double-fan adhesive bound instead, with a resulting cost saving.

- Economy-bind volumes 5/8" thick or less. See appendix C, Nonstandard Library Binding.

NOTES

[a] Either through the fold, oversewn, or side sewn, rather than adhesive bound.

[b] This occurs when a monograph has been disbound and the folds of the signatures repaired. Because such preparation is labor intensive, it is reserved for exceptional volumes.

[c] Oversewn and side-sewn volumes must occasionally be rebound because their cases have worn out or been damaged. If the volumes open well and have adequate margins, recase; if they open poorly, cut away the sewing structure and double-fan adhesive bind to improve functional characteristics. Volumes that must open and lie flat, e.g., music scores, should not be oversewn.

[d] Double-fan adhesive binding is usually reserved for volumes no more than 2" thick, but in cases where a text block is thicker and oversewing is not possible because of binding margins, double-fan adhesive bind as the option of last resort. If the job is well done, the volume is likely to be durable. To ensure optimal openability and durability, whenever possible limit the size of text blocks to 2" thick or less, regardless of the width of the binding margins.

*Decision Tree 3: **Binding Serials***

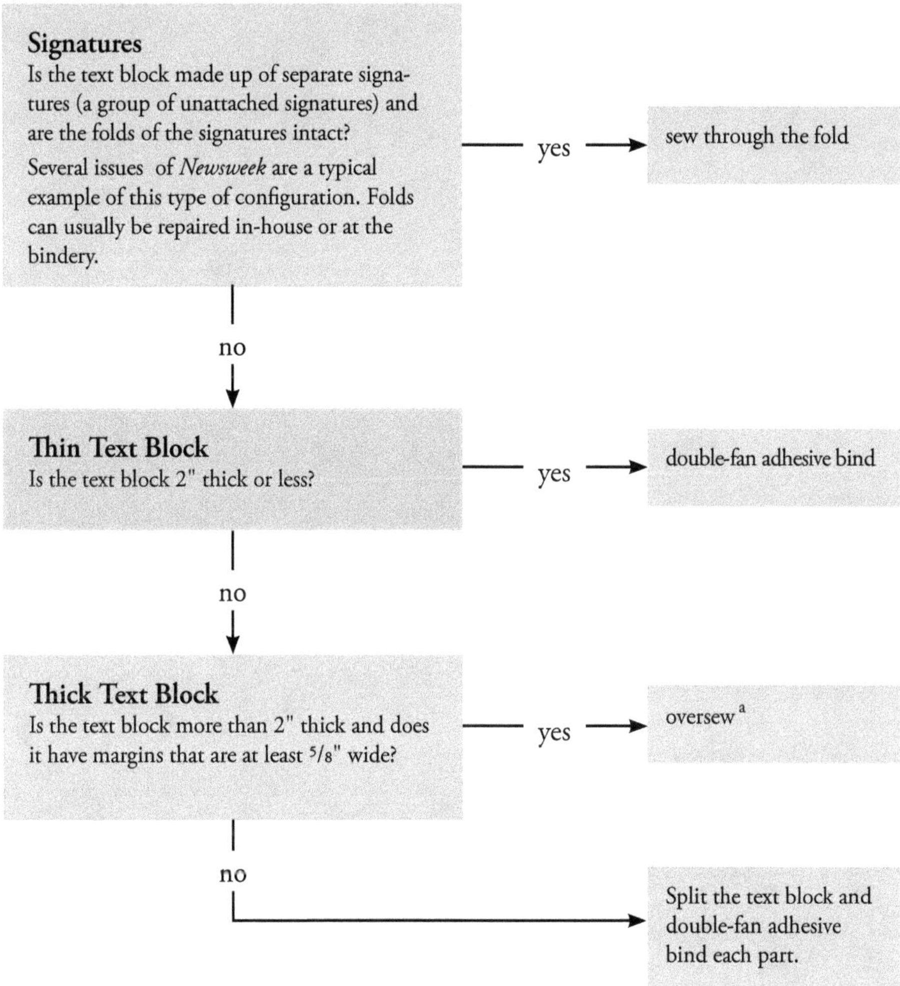

Cost-saving Option

- Reserve sewing through the fold for volumes that cannot be double-fan adhesive bound because milling the spine would damage the paper, remove already-narrow binding margins, or cut away plates that bleed to the inner edges of pages.

  Using these criteria, some volumes that are potential candidates for sewing through the fold would be double-fan adhesive bound instead, with a resulting cost savings.

NOTE

[a] To ensure optimal openability and durability, whenever possible limit the size of text blocks to 2" thick or less, regardless of the width of the binding margins. Volumes that must open and lie flat, music scores for example, should not be oversewn.

Appendix B

Inspecting Library Bound Volumes

1. Inspect the Unopened Volume

Spine Stamping

- Is the spine lettered correctly? If there is an error, was it made by the library or the binder?
- Are lines of lettering properly positioned? They should be parallel or perpendicular to the spine of the volume—not crooked.
- Horizontal lettering should not wrap onto the front or back board of the case.
- Are letters evenly impressed and crisp?

Covering Material

- Is the covering material clean and free from dust and gluey fingerprints?
- Is the cloth smoothly and completely adhered to both boards?
- Is the cloth free from large knots and scars?

Joints

- Are the joints (the grooves on either side of the spine) parallel to the spine and uniformly and adequately deep?

Rounding and Backing

- The *Standard* specifies exceptions to rounding and backing. Have these exceptions been made?
- In cases where the volume has been rounded and backed, is the spine of the text block properly shaped at both the head and tail? See figure 58.

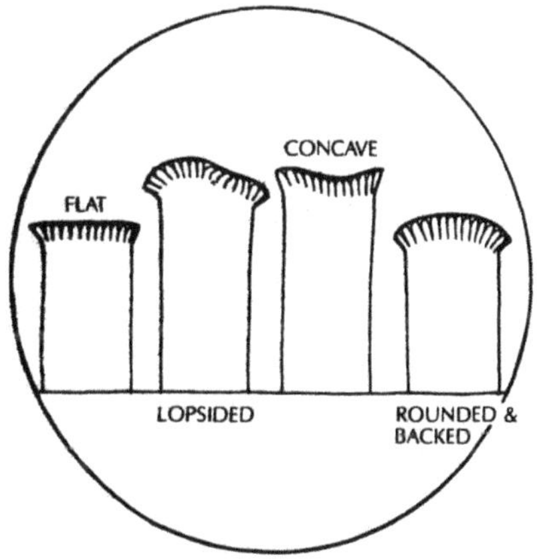

Figure 58. Examples of proper and improper spine shapes.

Squares

- Are the squares (i.e., the edges of the boards that extend beyond the text block at the head, fore edge, and tail) even, and of an acceptable width (1⁄16" to 3⁄16")?

Uneven squares may be a sign that the text block is not cased in tightly against the spine of the case. If the text block is left untrimmed, however, either in accordance with the library's specifications or to avoid cutting away text or illustrations, squares may be unavoidably irregular. If flush binding has been specified (i.e., if the volume is bound flush with the bottom of the case), there should be little or no square at the tail of the volume.

Edges of the Text Block

- Are the edges of the text block free from adhesive so that pages fan without restriction?
- If trimming has been specified by the library, are there major scratches and gouges across the edges of the text block, which would indicate deep nicks in the binder's guillotine blade?
- Has text been cut away? If yes, inspect the text block to determine whether the damage is significant.
- If the library has specified that the edges of the text be left untrimmed, have instructions been followed?

2. Inspect Spine Linings

- Open the volume to its approximate center; look down the hollow that forms between the spine of the text block and the spine of the case.

Spine Linings on *Standard* Bindings

- Is there a spine lining that extends to within ½" of the head and tail of the spine?

Spine Linings on Nonstandard Bindings

- Have the specifications agreed upon by the library and the bindery been followed regarding spine lining?

3. Inspect Board Surfaces

- Open the front cover, then the back cover, and inspect the inside surface of each board.

Endpapers

- Are the endpapers smoothly and completely adhered to the boards?
- Are the edges of the endpapers smooth and cut straight?
- On selected volumes, grasp the head of the front cover with one hand and the tail of the cover with the other. Bend the board gently back and forth perpendicular to the spine. If endpapers are not properly adhered, you will see a separation between endpaper and board.

Turn-ins

- Are the turn-ins (the margins of covering material that wrap onto the insides of the boards) uniform and approximately ⅝" wide?
- Are the edges of the covering material smooth and cut straight?

Spine Lining

- Does the spine lining extend onto each board at least 1"?
- Is the spine lining uniformly wide, head to tail, on each board?

4. Inspect Text Block

- Leaf through the text block; check the volume against instructions to the binder.

Special Instructions

- Have all instructions to the binder been followed, including such specifications as color of covering material, method of leaf attachment, treatment of the covers of paperbacks, and construction of pockets?

Endpapers

- Is the style of endpaper appropriate for the method of leaf attachment used?
- Have endpapers been attached according to specifications in the *Standard* and the library's binding profile?

Binding Margin between Endpapers and Text Block

- Check the volume between the endpapers and the first leaf of the text block, and between the endpapers and last leaf of the text block. For text blocks that have been double-fan adhesive bound, are the endpapers tipped no more than ¼" onto the facing leaf?
- Note that if the covers of paperbacks and serials are bound in, adhesive will on occasion inevitably seep into the text block to a depth of more than ¼". The stiffer the cover, the more likely this is to happen.
- For text blocks that have been recased, are the binding margins between endpapers and the first and last leaves of the text block neat and free from the residue of old spine lining?

Text Block

- Is the text block properly oriented in the case (i.e., is it right-side-up)? Are all leaves securely attached?
- Are leaves and serial issues in correct order?
- Have all paper repairs been made neatly and with appropriate materials? (If the library has a policy for making all repairs in-house, have paper tears been noted by the binder?)

- Has text near the binding margin been obscured by sewing, notching, or adhesive?
- Has text or have the folds of folded leaves been trimmed away?

5. Open and Lie Flat

- Determine whether the volume opens well and lies flat.

Ideally, all volumes should open well and lie flat. Most will, if an appropriate method of leaf attachment has been chosen. Stiff papers, however, create problems that sometimes cannot be compensated for by good decision making and technique. Papers may be stiff because they are thick, heavily coated or sized, laminated, or oriented such that the grain direction is perpendicular, rather than parallel, to the spine.

If a high percentage of volumes do not open well and lie flat, reevaluate the methods of leaf attachment specified by the library or the bindery, taking into consideration the problem of paper stiffness.

Appendix C

Nonstandard Library Binding

Many (if not most) library binders provide one or more styles of binding that do not meet the *Standard.* Some are less expensive than standard binding and some are simply different. This appendix focuses on binding styles that share many of the characteristics of standard library binding but lack one or more significant features, and it details cost savings commonly offered by library binders.

There are a number of reasons why libraries sometimes specify non-standard binding. Candidates for such treatment might include volumes that will be discarded within a relatively short period of time, incomplete serial volumes, volumes that are expected to receive extremely low use, or light-weight paperbacks. A library may even choose non-standard binding strictly as a cost-saving measure. The advantages of standard binding are sometimes sacrificed in the process. It is important that the librarian understand the full range of options available for non-standard binding and the implications of selecting each, so that appropriate treatment decisions can be made.

The cost of library binding can sometimes be reduced by eliminating certain steps in the binding process or by using materials that are less expensive than those specified in the *Standard.* The margin of savings is small, and the extra management and technology demands created when services are diversified can altogether offset cost savings. In addition, lower-grade materials sometimes cause costly production problems. A less compromising way to achieve cost savings is to limit or eliminate the special treatments asked of the bindery.

Reducing or Eliminating Choice of Leaf Attachment

Whereas *Standard* binding allows the library or binder to select from among five different methods of leaf attachment (recasing, sewing through the fold, double-fan adhesive binding, oversewing, and side sewing), economy binding typically involves the use of only one option—usually double-fan adhesive binding. As a consequence, librarians sometimes construe adhesive binding to be a cost-saving measure. While the cost of a well executed adhesive binding is indeed a bit lower than the cost of sewing, it is mainly the streamlining of procedures and elimination of options that save time and money.

Using Less-expensive Covering Materials

Alternatives to Group F buckram (the *Standard* material)

- Type II and other thin, light-weight covering material
- the original covers of paperbacks laminated between polyester film and paper, and
- covering material printed with a scan or photocopy of the original cover.

Some of these materials are more attractive and durable than others, but none has the fold and tear strength, abrasion resistance, and imperviousness to water and oils that characterize Group F buckram. A great deal can be learned about these cover materials by handling, abrading, and tearing samples.

There are certain categories of binding for which light-weight covering materials are well suited, for example, small and medium-sized paperbacks. The laminate formed by sandwiching an original paperback cover between polyester film and paper is popular for these because it preserves cover graphics and text. Such laminates, however, are inflexible and cause considerable stiffness in the hinge area of the case. Many binders also offer scanned and printed paperback covers for use in place of the originals. Printed covers also preserve the graphics, text, call numbers, barcodes, ownership stamps, and other library markup, and do not have the problems of the laminate sandwich. They are printed on paper that is strong and flexible.

Quarter Binding

Quarter binding (also known as LUM binding) is usually used only for serials. Rather than covering the entire case with buckram, as is specified in the *Standard,* a strip of buckram wraps over the spine of the volume only. It extends onto the front and back boards approximately one-quarter of the width of each board. The boards are otherwise bare. Although less covering material is used, unless a bindery does a significant amount of quarter binding, it is unlikely that savings will be realized. The procedure requires a separate work area and represents a departure from routine procedures. Any routine that disrupts regular work flow is costly. Furthermore, because the boards on quarter bindings are not fully covered with buckram, they tend to delaminate if volumes are heavily used. They also absorb excessive moisture in damp environments and may warp with changes in humidity. During library emergencies involving flooding, they absorb large quantities of water.

Restricting Spine-stamping Options

In *Standard* binding, lettering is restricted only by the height and width of the spine, and the number of stamping foils (black, white, and gold are available). Restrictions can be placed on lettering to control the cost of economy binding. These may include limiting the total number of characters that can be stamped on the spine, allowing only vertical placement of letters, and eliminating choice of foil color.

Pamphlet Binding

Too many types of pamphlet bindings are offered by binders to discuss them here in detail. The important points to consider are whether paper and board are alkaline, whether cloth is sturdy, and whether text blocks open well for easy reading and photocopying. Many pamphlet binding styles involve stapling through the side, which results in poor openability. Double-fan adhesive bound economy paperback bindings are often a better alternative. Single-signature pamphlets are typically stapled or machine- or hand-sewn through the fold into plain boards with cloth spines. They open well. Sewing is stronger than stapling because stitches secure text nearly the full length of the fold, while staples grip it only in a limited number of places. Sewing may involve additional cost.

Librarians should investigate the various types of cost-saving products offered by their binders using information in this appendix as a check list. A good understanding of standard materials and procedures, and the ways in which nonstandard bindings differ from them and from each other, is essential to determining whether certain types of volumes in the library's collections are appropriate candidates for binding in nonstandard ways.

Appendix D

Supplementary Bindery Products and Services

Some library binders provide products and services in addition to standard and nonstandard library binding. An assessment of the need for and quality of supplementary services must be made independently from an evaluation of mainstream library binding services. Strengths in one product line or service do not necessarily guarantee strengths in another. This section outlines some of the services currently provided by commercial library binders in the United States and Canada.

1. Construction of Protective Enclosures

Phase Boxes

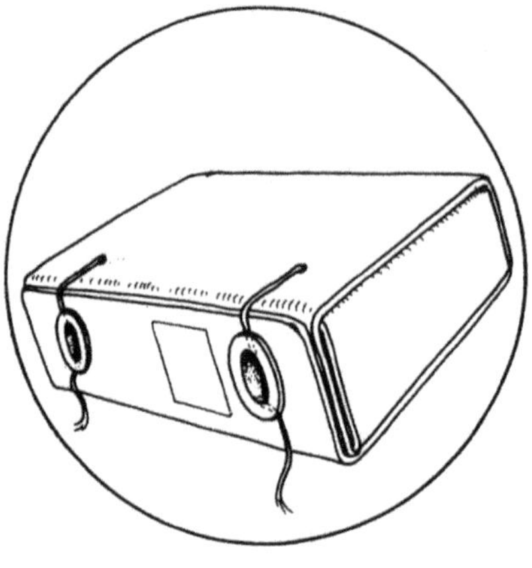

Figure 59a. A closed phase box.

Phase boxes were developed at the Library of Congress, where they were initially intended to function as the first "phase" in the preservation of worn or damaged volumes. See figure 59a. In fact, phase boxes have become a more-or-less permanent solution to many preservation problems, rather than an interim one. Phase boxes are an inexpensive means of providing library materials with protection from light, dust, mechanical damage; and rapid fluctuations in temperature and humidity. They can be used to house worn and damaged books and journals, groups of pamphlets or journal issues that cannot or should not be bound, books with accompanying maps and charts, music scores and parts that must be used separately but housed together, diskettes, CDs, DVDs, cassettes, scrolls, and a variety of other library materials that are otherwise difficult to protect and shelve.

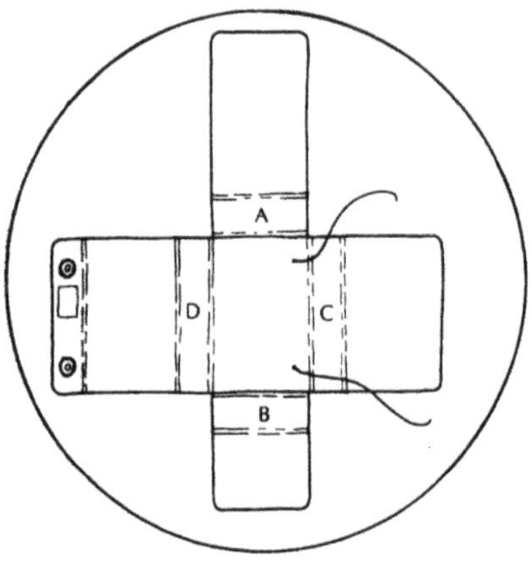

Figure 59b. An open phase box.

The term "phase box" is a bit of a misnomer: "wrapper" is a better descriptor. Phase boxes usually consist of two custom-cut strips of alkaline/buffered board, approximately .055" thick, crossed and adhered (the vertical strip inside the horizontal one) to form a two-ply rear board and four flaps. See figure 59b. These flaps wrap around the enclosed item(s) to provide firm support. Phase box designs vary slightly from binder to binder, as does the type of closure used to secure the flaps. Among the often-used closures are buttons-and-string, Velcro dots, and magnetic strips. Typed or computer-printed labels can be applied to the spines of phase boxes, or spines can be hot stamped. A more sturdy protective enclosure can be made by mounting a phase box onto the back board of a buckram-covered case that is constructed in the same way as the case for a library binding. See Sections 12.–12.6 of the *Standard.*

Binders often manufacture phase boxes using measurements supplied by the library, rather than requiring that volumes be sent to the bindery. Some binders even provide libraries with devices that, when properly used, ensure accurate measurement.

Double-tray Boxes

Double-tray boxes consist of two cloth-covered, paper-lined trays, one slightly larger than the other, and a case that is constructed in the same way as the case for a library binding. See Sections 12.–12.6 of the *Standard.* The smaller tray is mounted onto the inside of the back board of the case; the larger is mounted onto the inside of the front board. See figure 60. When the case is closed, one tray fits tightly inside the other. Materials used in construction vary greatly. Board ranges from binders board, as specified in Section 16.0 of the *Standard,* to high-quality mat board. Covering materials range from museum-quality light-weight book cloth to acrylic-coated buckram. Like phase boxes, double-tray boxes provide volumes with protection from light, dust, mechanical damage, and rapid fluctuations in temperature and humidity. They are more dimensionally stable than phase boxes, seal contents more completely, and are easier to open and close. They are far more difficult to construct and are more expensive.

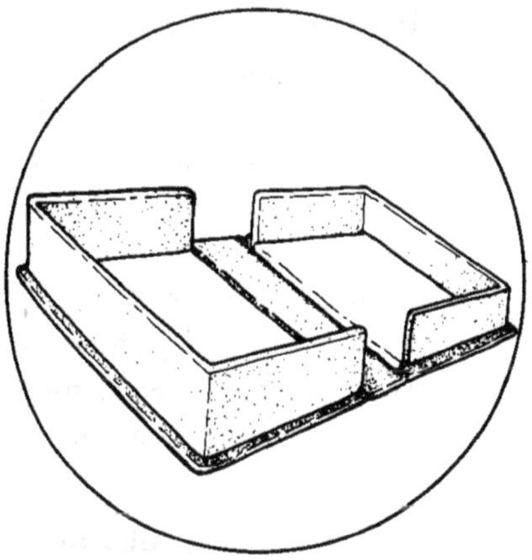

Figure 60. A double-tray box.

Double-tray boxes are typically used to house rare and valuable books, works of art such as prints and watercolors (matted or unmatted), manuscripts, plates, and photographic prints.

Machine-made Enclosures

In the 1990s plotting machines were developed that can cut and crease various kinds of board to produce enclosures to the exact dimensions specified. These boxes are constructed from a single piece of board that folds easily. In most cases the configuration is similar to a pizza box. The board is lightweight, fluted, and, of archival quality. Machine-made enclosures are less expensive than some others and are easy for library patrons to use. Structures such as lock-tab portfolios are appropriate for thinner volumes. Here, savings are achieved through use of less expensive but high quality material.

2. Reprographic Services

Preservation Facsimiles

An alternative to binding deteriorated paper is to create a paper facsimile. These are produced on photocopy machines, or more often today, using scanners and digital print engines. Facsimiles must be printed on paper that meets or exceeds *ANSI—Permanence of Paper for Printed Library Materials* (*ANSI/NISO Z39.48-1992 [R2002]*) or the most current edition of that standard. They can range from black-and-white photocopies to high-quality color digital prints.

The advantage of contracting for preservation facsimiles with library binders is that they are also able to provide complementary binding services.

Libraries are just beginning now to master the technical procedures required to ingest digital files created by binders, and to create the administrative descriptive and structural metadata required for archiving and online delivery.

3. Conservation Services

Deacidification

The correlation between acidity and paper deterioration is well known, and several binders offer deacidification services. At one time multiple processes were available commercially but that number has dwindled. Paper can be bathed in aqueous deacidification agents sheet by sheet or in batches; or bathed or sprayed in non-aqueous solutions. Before contracting for deacidification services, it is extremely important to evaluate the short- and long-term effectiveness as well as the risk to people and library materials of the specific processes under consideration. Request test data regarding safety and effectiveness and have that data evaluated by independent sources. Sample objects from each treated batch must also be tested. In cases where conservation protocols include chemical treatments, such as this one, it is wise to involve a conservator in all aspects of decision making and evaluation.

Polyester Encapsulation

Polyester encapsulation involves sandwiching paper between two sheets of inert polyester film and sealing the edges of the film using double-sided tape, a heat welder, or an ultrasonic welder. While use of double-sided tape was once very popular, it has been observed that an object can shift inside its capsule and come into contact with adhesive that seeps out from under the edges of double-sided tape. Heat and ultrasonic welding eliminate all use of adhesives. Polyester encapsulation protects paper from breaking, tearing, moisture, dirt, grease, and other potential hazards. Brittle paper, when encapsulated, can be handled safely. The treatment can be reversed simply by cutting away the weld that seals the polyester sandwich. Encapsulated sheets can be stored in map cases, housed in boxes, or bound. Materials such as frequently handled prints, posters, manuscripts, and maps are sometimes appropriate candidates for encapsulation, although it is important to confer with a conservator regarding potential mechanical and chemical damage. Original manuscripts, maps and artwork may have friable media (e.g., charcoal or pastels), which should not come in direct contact with polyester film or any other surface.

There is some controversy about whether acidic paper should be encapsulated without being deacidified, the thinking being that polyester does not allow the harmful by-products of deteriorating paper to be released. Some research has suggested that encapsulating a sheet of alkaline paper together with the acidic item will compensate for the reportedly negative effects of encapsulation. An alternative is to deacidify items before encapsulating. Because of uncertainties in this regard, librarians should consult with conservators before making the decision to encapsulate rare and valuable items.

Special Cover Treatments

In cases where the cover text or art is important to a paperback, the library may choose to remove the cover and retain it in conjunction with a standard binding. Paperback covers can be mounted on the hard cover of the bound volume. This is sometimes impractical because

a) the paper cover has a front panel and folded, book-jacket-style flap, or

b) the cover has important information front and back.

If the text block is recased or double-fan adhesive bound, the front and rear paperback covers may be hinged onto the text block with "archival" tape. Covers can also be hinged in with Japanese paper and paste, but this is best accomplished in the library.

Conservation Binding and Flat Paper Treatment

Additional conservation services are offered by library binders but their nature and appropriate application exceed the scope of this document.

Appendix E

Key Elements of a Binding Agreement

Because the relationship between a library and a library bindery is complex, it can be useful to develop a written document that states expectations clearly and succinctly. Such a document is sometimes mandated, particularly in government-supported institutions. The process of drawing up a binding agreement or contract provides the librarian with an opportunity to assess and articulate a library's binding needs and priorities. In addition, such a document can serve as a starting point for discussions when a library first begins to work with a binder. This appendix contains components that are basic to most binding agreements and contracts:

1. Service Specifications

Scope

- What units of the library are covered by the agreement?
- For how long will the agreement be effective?
- Does the library have the option to renew or extend the agreement? For how long?
- How many serials does the library anticipate binding during each year of the agreement?
- How many monographs?

Price

- Can the binder's prices be raised or lowered during the period defined by the agreement? Under what circumstances?
- Who is authorized to request, and who to approve, price changes?
- Are pick-up, transportation, and delivery costs included in net binding prices?

Compliance with Specifications

- For what comparable institutions does the bindery now provide services?
- From whom can references be secured at each institution?
- What is the square footage of the bindery?
- How many people are employed?

- How many adhesive-binding, sew-through-the-fold, and oversewing machines are in use?
- What sample bindings must be submitted to the library for evaluation?
- What sample forms (e.g., binding slips, packing slips)?
- Is the binder permitted to subcontract work with the approval of the library?
- What constitutes grounds for termination of the agreement between library and bindery?
- With what technical specifications is the bindery required to comply?
- Can the library request alternative procedures in special cases? How will such requests be communicated?
- If the bindery cannot comply with the specifications provided for a particular volume, how shall it proceed?

Insurance and Security

- For how much shall each binding shipment be insured?
- At what point in the work flow is the binder expected to assume responsibility for library materials in transit from library to bindery?
- At what point does this responsibility end?
- How shall the binder compensate the library for lost or damaged materials?
- By what means shall the bindery prove that it carries adequate insurance?

Communication

- How often and when shall staff from the library be allowed to visit the bindery?
- How often shall a representative of the bindery visit the library?
- What binding-related knowledge and skills must the bindery representative have?
- To what extent shall the bindery provide training for library staff, and what is the expected nature of that training?

Packing, Pick-up, and Delivery

- How shall the library separate materials for packing in preparation for sending them to the bindery?
- Who shall provide shipping boxes and other supplies?
- Will the bindery transport materials in company-operated vehicles?
- Are other arrangements acceptable?
- How often shall the bindery pick up materials at the library?
- What is the anticipated turnaround time for regular and rush shipments?

- Where shall materials be picked up and delivered?
- How shall the library compensate the bindery in cases where materials must be picked up or delivered to alternative sites?
- What documentation is the library prepared to provide with each binding shipment?

Errors and Delays

- How shall binding errors be handled by the library and the binder?
- Within what period of time must corrections be made?
- Who shall absorb the cost of making corrections, shipping where necessary, and replacing damaged volumes?
- Shall replacement costs include the cost of searching, ordering, and processing replacements?
- How shall the binder compensate the library in cases where materials are returned to the library late, without prior notice?

Uniform Binding of Serials and Sets

- What mechanism does the binder have for matching the binding pattern, placement of lettering on the spine, and color of stamping foil and cloth for volumes that are a part of a serial, set, or series?
- If the account is new, within what time frame must the binder establish a data file of binding patterns for the library?

Computer Services

- What computerized services and computer-generated reports must the binder provide the library?

Invoices

- How soon after a shipment of materials is sent to the bindery must the binder present the library with an invoice?
- What information shall invoices include?
- How many copies of the invoice are required by the library?

2. Technical Specifications

While the *Standard* is composed of fairly complete technical specifications, there is no simple road map to good binding. A variety of treatment options are presented, from which the library must choose. Several issues should be addressed in a binding agreement.

Collation

- Shall periodicals receive custom or standard collation? If the custom collation desired differs from the process described in the *Standard,* exactly how shall materials be collated?

Repair

- Should paper tears be mended by the binder? If so, with what materials should repairs be made? If not, how should the binder handle a volume with torn leaves?

Leaf Attachment

- In the absence of specific instructions, what guidelines shall the binder use for selecting a method of leaf attachment? See, for example, appendix A of this *Guide.*
- Which endpaper shall be used for each method of leaf attachment, and how shall the endpaper be attached?
- Should single signatures be sewn through the fold by hand, or can they be machine sewn?
- Is side sewing allowed?

Trimming

- When shall the text blocks of monographs be trimmed, and when shall they be left untrimmed?
- When shall the text blocks of serials be trimmed, and when shall they be left untrimmed?

Rounding and Backing

- What exceptions, if any, in addition to those listed in the *Standard,* should the binder make to the specification that all volumes shall be rounded and backed?

Making the Case and Casing in

- When, if ever, is it acceptable for the binder to use a wide hinge when constructing a case?
- When, if ever, should a text block be bound flush with the bottom of the case?

Stamping the Covering Material

- How shall lettering (author, title, call number, volume information) be oriented on the spines of volumes, and where shall it be printed in cases where it does not fit on the spine?
- What color stamping foil shall be used?

Special Handling

- Must the library receive copies of binding slips for each volume bound? If so, should the slips be attached to text blocks, or left unattached?
- Should security devices be applied by the binder? If so, where on volumes should they be placed?
- Are any special procedures required for volumes that have barcodes?

Nonstandard Products and Services

- What products and services does the library require that are not specified in the *Standard?*
- What are the specifications for each of these products and services?

Appendix F

Bindery Customer Profile

This customer profile is a sample working tool developed for bindery customers so that (except in special cases) they can prepare volumes for binding without including repetitive instructions on binding slips. The customer profile contains general and specific information on bindery services, technical options, and the library's binding policy.

The profile streamlines library and bindery operations, reduces questions and errors, and allows a library to tailor its binding program to meet local needs. These working tools should be reviewed and updated regularly.

Bindery Customer Profile

CONTACT INFORMATION	
SHIP/DELIVER TO	BILL TO
Customer	Customer
Address	Address
Contact person	Contact person
Phone	Phone
Email	Email

Shipment Cycle	☐ 4 weeks	☐ 2 weeks	☐ 1 week	☐ other

GENERAL INSTRUCTIONS			
Periodicals*	☐ custom	☐ standard	☐ economy
Books*	☐ custom	☐ standard	☐ economy
Paperbacks*	☐ custom	☐ standard	☐ economy
* unless noted otherwise on binding slip			
Brittle volumes	☐ return unbound	☐ construct phase box	☐ reformat
Questions	☐ return unbound	☐ use judgement	☐ call
Barcodes	☐ bind as is	☐ remove	☐ return
Insert security devices	☐ all volumes ☐ library supplied	☐ periodicals only ☐ bindery supplied	☐ books only
Binding slip	☐ attach	☐ leave loose	☐ do not return
Incomplete volumes	☐ bind as is	☐ return unbound	
Uneven issues	☐ trim; stub	☐ trim; no stub	☐ bind as is
Periodicals too thick	☐ bind as is ☐ call	☐ split	☐ return unbound
Volume with issues/ pages to be inserted	☐ tip in, where possible	☐ rebind only	
Mending	☐ only where necessary for binding ☐ do not mend; bind as is and flag	☐ all paper tears ☐ do not mend; flag and return unbound	☐ do not mend; bind as is
Trimming	☐ if margins are greater than ¼" ☐ all volumes	☐ periodicals only ☐ no volumes	☐ books only
Preferred leaf attachment	☐ follow binding slip ☐ follow customer's guidelines in order of preference: _ recase _ oversew	☐ follow binder's guidelines _ sew through fold _ side sew	 _ double-fan adhesive bind

profile continued next page

BINDERY CUSTOMER PROFILE (p. 2)

If unable to recase	☐ make minor repairs (if possible) and recase ☐ disbind and sew through fold	☐ return unbound	☐ double fan adhesive bind
Bind flush with the bottom of the case	☐ volumes over 2" thick	☐ periodicals only	☐ all volumes
CUSTOM PERIODICAL COLLATION			
Covers of periodical issues	☐ bind as is ☐ remove back covers only	☐ remove stiff covers only	☐ remove front and back covers
Advertisements	☐ remove unpaged ads at the front and back of each issue ☐ bind as is	☐ remove unpaged ads	☐ remove paged and unpaged ads
Supplements	☐ bind as is	☐ bind at the back of the volume	
Contents	☐ bind after title page at front of volume	☐ bind as is	
Indexes	☐ bind at back of volume ☐ remove individual indexes	☐ bind at front of volume	☐ bind as is
Title pg., content, and index if they can't be divided	☐ bind as is	☐ bind at back of volume	☐ bind at front of volume
BOOK COLLATION			
Paper covers	☐ remove ☐ mount front covers	☐ remove stiff covers only	☐ bind as is
SPINE STAMPING			
Print color	☐ white	☐ gold	☐ follow binding slip
Imprint	☐ all volumes ☐ follow binding slip Example Abbreviated example	☐ periodicals only	☐ books only
Binding slip instructions	☐ follow binding slip exactly as typed	☐ follow binder's format for placement of title and variable information	☐ follow computer pattern
Call numbers	☐ all volumes	☐ books only	☐ no call numbers* * allow 2" at tail of spine

profile continued next page

Bindery Customer Profile (p. 3)

Call number position (order of preference)

Position:	__ horizontal (begin 2" from tail of spine)		__ vertical
	__ lower-left front cover	__ upper-left front cover	__ omit call number
Call number on spine in all cases:	__ binder shortens title	__ title on front cover	__ title can be omitted

Position of title and variable information for periodicals (order of preference)

Position:	__ horizontal	__ vertical	__ front cover, flush left
Year format	☐ 2005-2006	☐ 2005-06	☐ 2005/06
Book-format	☐ author first	☐ title first	☐ follow binding slip
Break lines	☐ follow binding slip	☐ allow 2 spaces	☐ use bold line
Head and tail lines	☐ double lines ☐ special lines	☐ single lines	☐ bold lines

SPECIAL INSTRUCTIONS

Parts of a Bound Volume

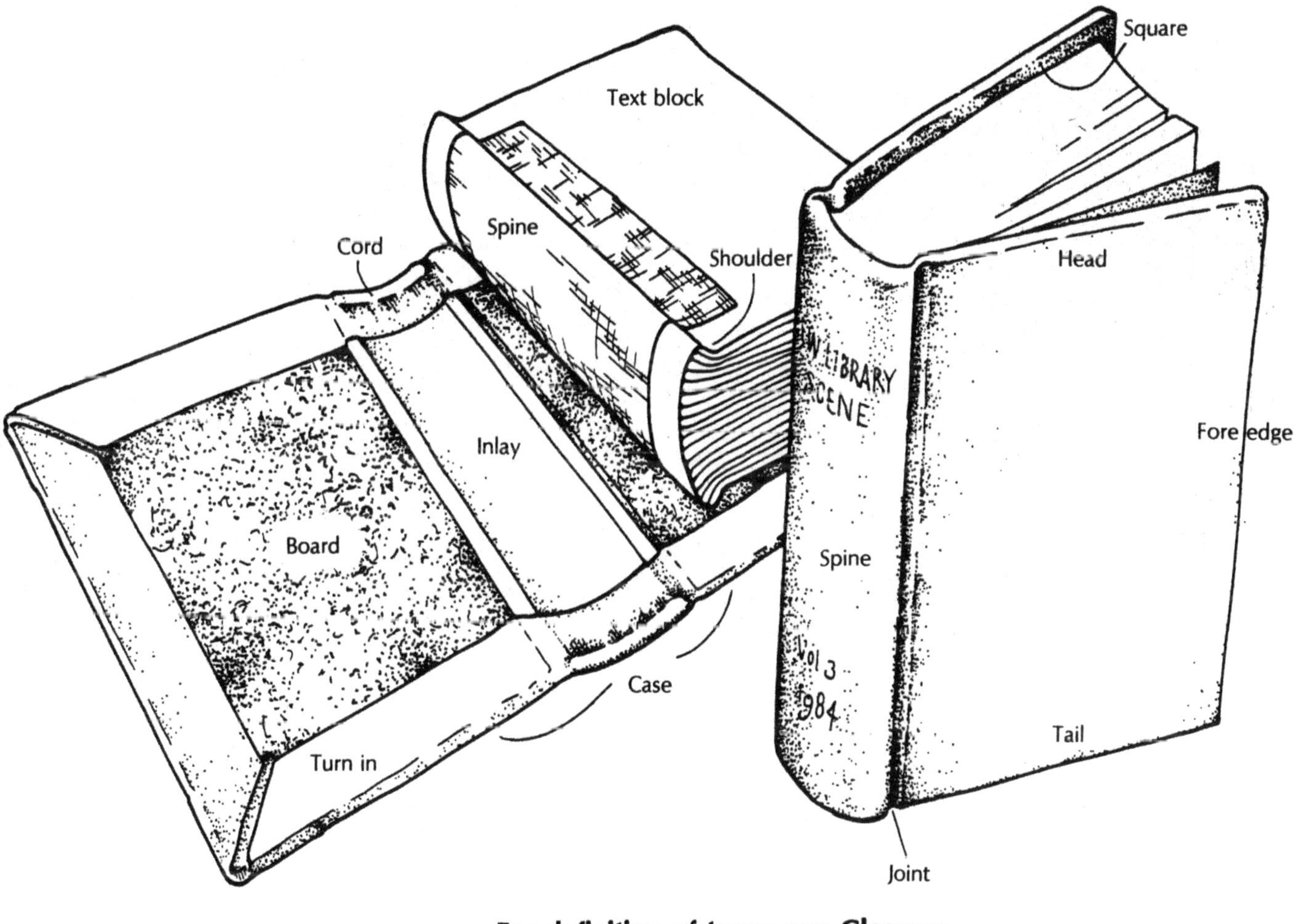

For definition of terms see Glossary.

Illustrations by Gary Frost

Printed in the USA
CPSIA information can be obtained
at www.ICGtesting.com
JSHW051816170923
48377JS00007B/37

9 780838 984840